Moral Principles
and Political Obligations

Moral Principles
and Political Obligations

A. John Simmons

Princeton University Press
Princeton, New Jersey

Published by Princeton University Press, Princeton, New Jersey
In the United Kingdom: Princeton University Press, Oxford

ALL RIGHTS RESERVED

Library of Congress Cataloging in Publication Data will be
found on the last printed page of this book

This book has been composed in VIP Melior

Clothbound editions of Princeton University Press books
are printed on acid-free paper, and binding materials are
chosen for strength and durability.

Printed in the United States of America by Princeton
University Press, Princeton, New Jersey

First *Princeton Paperback* printing, 1981

9 8 7 6 5 4 3

CONTENTS

PREFACE

It is in a way remarkable that the problem of political obligation continues to puzzle political philosophers. That it is a "core" problem has seemed obvious to thinkers of many different times and persuasions. Certainly the liberal tradition in political theory has continued to stress its importance over many centuries. The classical political treatises of Hobbes, Locke, Rousseau, and Kant all display the centrality of the problem of political obligation quite clearly. Nor have contemporary writers overlooked it. Yet in spite of this, it is difficult today to find two philosophers who even agree on a basic approach to the problem, let alone on its solution.

There are, no doubt, many reasons for this apparent lack of progress toward an accepted result. Surely the absence of agreement on any general theory of justification in ethics is responsible for much of the confusion. And the distressing inadequacies of consent and contract theories (on which much of the liberal political tradition is built) have led to a great deal of aimless wandering. But equally important in this respect have been the philosopher's insistence on regarding the problem as rather simpler than it is, his failure to examine the full range of possible solutions to the problem, and his refusal to make clear from the start what could count as a genuine solution to the problem.

This essay is an attempt to understand and answer the ancient questions about political obligation in a way which I hope will strike the reader as careful and systematic. A successful effort in this area would, of course, be important to political philosophers. But I hope that my arguments and conclusions will be of interest to others as well, for we all surely have a common stake in these matters. Only a very unusual man will have never at least seriously considered disobeying the law. And while dis-

obedience is often a relatively trivial matter of convenience, this is not always so. Disobedience in the name of
widely shared moral values or fundamental political
principles is also a commonplace. It is natural in such
contexts to wonder if our relationship to our government
constrains us to obey, or if such (real or imagined) political bonds can be voided or overridden by competing
moral considerations. Few of us doubt that disobedience
is at least sometimes justifiable, but we may wonder if
there is a moral presumption in favor of obedience, which
can be overcome only in cases of obvious or prolonged injustice or oppression. Have we a moral obligation to obey
the law, or are we merely "obliged" to do so by the threat
of legal sanctions? Because moral obligations are taken
seriously by most of us, the answer to such questions will
influence our attitudes toward our political and legal
authorities and institutions. If a clear and satisfactory
account of our political bonds can be given, the results
should be of interest to nonphilosophers and directly relevant to their conception of the ties which may exist between them and the political institutions of their countries of residence.

Accordingly, I have tried in this essay to present the
basic positions, the main lines of argument, and the important conclusions clearly and directly, with as little use
as possible of technical jargon. Because this book is intended as a contribution to moral and political philosophy, of course, there will be references and arguments
which nonphilosophers may find perplexing or unil-
luminating. But these should not prevent the primary
force of my presentations from being appreciated by any
careful reader. Parts of Chapters I, II, and III are specifically introductory in character, and should be especially
useful to those who are new to the subject. Sections I.i,
I.iii, II.i, and III.i, for instance, include arguments which
will already be familiar to many philosophers. But because discussions of these matters are essential preliminaries to the arguments which follow, I encourage

even my philosophical audience not to pass over these sections entirely.

There is, of course, a great deal of literature (not all of it philosophical) on the problem of political obligation; and while it would be both vain and foolish to ignore it, I can-not possibly do justice to all of it in this essay. I discuss many of the most important presentations in the text, often beginning my own arguments with an examination of the work of others. But many other useful works go unmentioned. A reasonably complete list of these is included in the Bibliography. In spite of the volume of literature on the problem, however, I am convinced that as yet no adequate job has been done in handling the topic of political obligation. Many treatments are simply too compressed and incomplete to be useful, appearing in the context of a discussion of some other issue (like civil disobedience or democratic government). Many others derive their conclusions only by way of background theories (e.g., linguistic or justificatory) which are not at all convincing. What is lacking almost throughout is a careful presentation of the problem's complexities conjoined with an analysis of the moral principles which might account for the ground of political obligation.

A major part of this essay will be devoted to my examination of a set of principles of duty and obligation. For one can only plausibly maintain that political obligation falls (or does not fall) under a particular moral principle, if one demonstrates that the principle actually applies (or does not apply) to citizens in normal political environments. And such a demonstration presupposes an adequate account of the conditions which must obtain for the duty or obligation to arise. Thus, we often read that political obligation is grounded in the consent of the governed (especially tacit consent), or in considerations of fairness, or gratitude; and we expect an analysis of the moral principles being appealed to. Yet such analyses are strikingly absent from the literature on political obligation, and surely in their absence no conclusions about political ob-

ligation can be drawn. I have tried to make a (long over-
due) start toward remedying this difficulty. Chapters IV
through VII include analyses of those moral principles
which can most reasonably be expected to yield accounts
of political obligation. The treatments of tacit consent, fair
play, and gratitude here presented are, I believe, important as substantial efforts to finally appreciate the conditions under which the moral requirements in question can
arise. I do not pretend, of course, that these treatments are
complete; much more remains to be said about these
moral principles, particularly the principles of fair play
and gratitude. I have tried to carry my analysis as far as
necessary for the completion of my main argument, while
at the same time acknowledging brevity as a desideratum.
The end aimed for is a book which is convincing, but un-
cluttered and of readable length. In this spirit, the exami-
nations of the moral principles undertaken here are designed only to allow me to reach conclusions about the
force of the corresponding accounts of political obligation, and, finally, to defend a general conclusion about the
problem of political obligation in Chapter VIII.

This book originated in a doctoral dissertation, accepted by the faculty of Cornell University in 1977, and
my first thanks must go to the supervisor of that dissertation, David Lyons. His careful criticism and numerous
suggestions for improvement have made the resulting
book a far better piece of work than it would otherwise
have been. Nicholas Sturgeon and Carl Ginet also read
and helped me to revise the dissertation. Many other individuals, especially among the students and faculty of
Cornell University and the University of Virginia, made
helpful suggestions in discussion concerning particular
arguments or sections of this essay. I hope that those
whose assistance I have forgotten will understand the
limits of recollection in such matters. Joel Feinberg and
Amy Gutmann read and commented on the whole of the
revised manuscript; I am grateful for their help. Throughout the time this was being written, my good friend David

Reeve listened patiently to my views on the problem of political obligation. His responses were invariably insightful, and the moral support he provided during hard times was invaluable. The production of this essay was also aided, in a different way, by Thomas Scanlon, who first interested me in the problem of political obligation, and by Thomas Nagel, who directed my first serious work on the topic. To all these friends I am grateful, though not all will be happy to see the poor use I have made of their advice. The mistakes which remain in spite of their assistance are, of course, my own responsibility.

A small part of Chapter III (in section i) and a large part of Chapter IV (sections i, ii, and iii) are revised versions of material previously published as "Tacit Consent and Political Obligation," in *Philosophy and Public Affairs* 5 (Spring 1976). Portions of Chapter V appeared in "The Principle of Fair Play," *Philosophy and Public Affairs* 8 (Summer 1979). Among those who provided help on these papers were David Lyons, David Reeve, Terence Irwin, John Marshall, Cora Diamond, Thomas Scanlon, and the editors of *Philosophy and Public Affairs*. I must also thank Gretchen Kossack, who typed the bulk of the manuscript, and the University of Virginia, which provided a small grant to cover the costs of preparing the manuscript for publication. Finally, I cannot overlook the support and encouragement I received from my wife Jean and daughter Shawn, which, though less direct than that already mentioned, was not less substantial.

Charlottesville, Virginia
May 1979

Moral Principles
and Political Obligations

INTRODUCTION

As Kurt Baier notes, "traditionally, the problem of political obligation has been construed as the problem of whether there is any such thing."[1] Also traditionally, there are at least three central areas of disagreement in attempts to solve the problem, as a result of the various answers which have been given to three basic questions: To whom is this obligation owed? What is this obligation an obligation to do? How does one come to be under this obligation? All of these questions, and suggested answers to them, will be discussed in the chapters to follow. But at least a general preliminary discussion will be useful at the start.

First, the problem of political obligation does not concern a number of things we might call "political obligations." It does not concern the politician's obligation to keep his campaign promises, the union member's obligation to vote in the national election in a certain way, or the tourist's "obligation" to defend his home country against foreign slander. It is at least clear that political obligation is supposed to be a moral requirement to act in certain ways in matters political. If anyone at all has this obligation, it is some (or all) members of some (or all) organized political communities. Many people feel, I think, that they are tied in a special way to their government, not just by "bonds of affection," but by *moral* bonds. While they complain loudly and often, and not without justification, of the shortcomings of government, they feel that they are nonetheless bound to support their country's political institutions and obey its laws, in ways that they are not bound to the corresponding institutions of *other* countries. Yet it is difficult to give any substance to this feeling of a special moral bond. It seems to me that the problem of political obligation is precisely the problem of explaining the nature and scope of such special moral bonds (if any such exist), and of determining who, if anyone, is constrained by them.

In taking this view of the problem, of course, I concur with the classical approach of the contract theorist, who stresses the need to understand the relationship or transaction which could create a moral bond between citizen and state. It is difficult to see how the problem could be characterized in any other way. Yet there are some who deny that political obligation is a kind of *moral* obligation. Thomas McPherson, for instance, makes such a denial a primary focus of his discussion of political obligation.[2] McPherson is not particularly clear about the status or character of his "non-moralised" political obligations, but I am inclined to believe that the word "obligation" cannot meaningfully be employed to refer to anything which is neither a moral obligation nor an institutional requirement (or what I will call a "positional duty" in I.iii). If by "political obligation" we mean simply some institutional requirement (i.e., the content of a "requiring rule" of that institution), then questions about political obligation can be answered by simple studies of political (or legal) institutions. This not only makes the questions rather unexciting and removes them from the proper field of inquiry for political philosophy (as opposed to political science), but it is clearly *not* what traditional formulations of the problem of political obligation have intended. Institutional requirements may, of course, be relevant to the problem properly understood, insofar as they are believed to have *moral* weight. I deal with this possibility in I.iii. I will not, then, consider McPherson's claims seriously beyond my treatment of institutional requirements, and will continue to regard political obligations as moral requirements of the ordinary sort.

Let me begin to be more specific about the nature of political obligations. Political obligation is closely linked with the obligation to obey some legitimate political authority, and insofar as that authority operates through laws, with the obligation to obey the law. In fact, many writers on this subject have suggested that the obligation to obey the law is precisely what we are looking for in asking about political obligation. But I think that to allow this would be to limit prematurely our inquiry. For political obligation has always been very intimately associated with the notion of citizenship, and has often been thought of as something like an obligation to be a "good citizen," in some fairly minimal sense. This includes, of course, more than just obeying the law; it includes supporting the political institutions of the state in other ways as well. For instance, I think that doing one's share in the defense of one's country, whether or not this is required by law, is generally taken to be an important aspect of one's political bonds. As a first approximation, then, we might say that a political obligation is an obligation to "support and comply with" (to use John Rawls's phrase) the political institutions of one's country of residence. This is vague, of necessity, but it will serve as a starting point. Depending on how we take this obligation to be generated, of course, this vague formula will be filled in to some extent. If the obligation is seen as arising from a contract, say, the content of the obligation will be specified by the terms of the contract. But an obligation which does not conform to this formula to at least a reasonable extent will not be one that we will want to call a "political obligation."

These remarks have cast some light on the second question, namely, "what is this obligation an obligation to do?" What of our other two questions? In response to the first question (i.e., "to whom is this obligation owed?"), we can point to three answers which seem to have attracted the most support: (a) the "governors" of the state (i.e., some set of government officials), (b) the government (as a set of political institutions), and (c) one's fellow citizens. But these three answers point, of course, to different conceptions of the grounds of political obligation (the concern of the third question, "how does one come to be under this obligation?"). So the "to whom" questions, questions about the *obligee*, will be answered only in answering the "how" questions, questions about the *grounds*. And these answers about grounds will fill out our answers to the "what" questions, questions about the *content* of the obligation, as I suggested earlier. Each conception of the ground of political obligation, then, carries its own account of the content and obligee for that obligation. And for that reason, we cannot attempt to answer our three questions in any more than a very general way at this point. We will, of course, be examining the most promising sets of answers as we proceed.

I do not intend, however, to begin immediately my examination of the possibilities for explaining the ground of a moral bond between the citizen and his government (or the institutions which are components of it). An important preliminary task is to state more clearly what an obligation is, and to explain the importance of institutional requirements. Chapter I will be devoted to that fundamental task, as a preparation for our discussion of the special duties and obligations which are our main concern. Chapter II will focus our examination more sharply on the problem of political obligation. There we will explain the limits on and standards for successful completion of our study, and look at several abortive attempts to solve the problem. With Chapter III, the discussion of the main lines of argument begins.

CHAPTER I

Obligations

I.i. Obligations and Final Judgments

Political obligation is, first and foremost, a special kind of *obligation*; and an obligation is a *requirement*. The fact that obligations (and duties) are requirements seems to set them apart from other moral considerations in a way which can hardly escape notice. Obligations are limitations on our freedom, impositions on our will, which must be discharged regardless of our inclinations. This is not, of course, to say that one cannot want to discharge an obligation (as when one has promised to take a beautiful woman out for the evening), but rather only that obligations, as requirements, are independent of our desires to perform or not. The fact that obligations are requirements accounts for the intimate tie between the concept of obligation (and less so, of duty) and the notions of force and coercion which we associate with it. For to be "required" to act seems always to involve, at the very least, a serious pressure to perform. This connection with pressure and coercion has seemed to many to be the salient feature of an obligation.[1]

But to say that an obligation (or a duty) is a requirement is not to say, as it might at first seem, that the existence of an obligation establishes an absolute moral claim on our action, or that obligations override all other sorts of moral considerations. Perhaps we can see this best by contrasting judgments of obligation with other sorts of moral judgments. Thus, we can contrast (a) "X has an obligation to do A" (and [b] "X has a duty to do A") with judgments like (c) "X ought to do A," (d) "It would be wrong for X not to do A," and (e) "A is the right thing for X to do."

It has been a commonplace in the history of moral philosophy to assume that these five judgments are all simply different ways of expressing the same thing.[2] And certainly the looseness and inconsistencies of ordinary moral discourse do often result in their free substitution for one another. But it also seems clear that in their central or standard uses, judgments of obligation (and duty) play a special role in moral discourse, to be distinguished from the roles of other sorts of moral judgments.[3] This special role can be seen most clearly in those cases which Lemmon has called "moral dilemmas."[4] Imagine, for instance, the case in which Dr. Jones promises to speak at an A.M.A. dinner on Saturday, only to hear while packing on Friday that an epidemic has struck a nearby town. Jones clearly has an obligation to appear at the dinner, but thousands may die unless he helps in the town. There is hardly any question about what Jones ought to do (or what is the right thing for Jones to do), and it is *not* what he has an *obligation* to do (although he may or may not have another obligation to help in the city, depending on how seriously we regard his "medical oaths"). The point, of course, is that "X has an obligation to do A" and "X ought to do A" (or "A is the right thing for X to do") cannot be simply different ways of expressing the same thing, since here we have a case in which a man has an obligation which he ought not to discharge. And further, "X has an obligation to do A" does not even *entail* that "X ought to do A."

Similarly, a case of conflicting obligations may arise. Suppose that Jones promises to take Jill to dinner whenever she wishes and also promises to take Joan to the theater on Friday. But on Thursday Jill calls to say that she wants to go to dinner on Friday. Jones will now have two obligations which cannot both be discharged. But the question remains open as to what Jones ought to do; and whatever Jones ought to do, it will involve failing to meet at least one of his obligations. So again we see that "X has an obligation to do A" does not entail that "X ought to do A." And we can easily see that there is no entailment in the other direction (i.e., from "ought" to "obligation") either. For (as Feinberg has argued),[5] it may well be true that Jones ought to give a match to the stranger who politely requests one (and that this is the right thing to do), without it being true that Jones has any obligation or duty to do so. Once again, this points to a difference in the ways in which "ought," "right," "duty," and "obligation" are used.

It would, of course, be foolish to insist that any of these terms is always used in one way or another, but certain facts about their characteristic uses seem clear; and in terms of these uses, we can separate judgments of duty and obligation from the other sorts of judgments we have discussed. When we tell a person that he has an obligation (or a duty) to do A, we are normally informing him that he stands in a certain relation to another person (or persons) and that there is a good reason (of a special sort) for him to do A. But when we tell him that he ought to do A, we are characteristically giving him *advice*,[6] and telling him that the strongest reasons there are for his acting favor doing A. "Ought-judgments" are often the end products of deliberation, in the course of which many factors may be considered, duties and obligations possibly among them. And of course such deliberation may be conducted from many points of view. We may want to know what an individual ought to do, considering only his own best interests, say, or considering only the good of his country, etc. This fact has led some writers to say that there are many different "senses" of "ought," such as the moral, prudential, and technical "senses." I do not find such claims particularly attractive.[a] But regardless of how we feel about

[a] The point of view from which we judge that "X ought to do A" does not seem to be part of the *meaning* of the word "ought." My views on this problem follow closely those of Harry Beran in "Ought, Obligation, and Duty," *Australasian Journal of Philosophy* 50 (December 1972). See also Russell Grice, *The Grounds of Moral Judgement*, Cambridge University Press, 1967, pp. 24-25. For a contrasting view, see Gilbert Harman, *The Nature of Morality*, Oxford University Press, 1977, pp. 59, 84-87, 118-124.

proliferating "senses," the fact remains that the most common use of "ought" does not assume a particular viewpoint, but rather conveys advice "all things considered" (this "all things considered" use of "ought" is commonly referred to as ought's "moral sense").

This is the most obvious difference between judgments of obligation and duty, and the other sorts of judgments considered. To say that an individual has an obligation or a duty is never, by itself, to offer a conclusive reason for his acting in a certain way. It is merely to report a good reason for acting, which may be outweighed by other considerations. But our judgments that the individual "ought to do A," that "A is the right thing for him to do," or that "it would be wrong for him not to do A," are all commonly "all things considered" judgments, ways of saying that when all reasons for action (or inaction) are considered, A has the weightiest reasons favoring it. We are unmoved by the Nazi officer's pleas, even if we believe that he did have a duty to obey his superior's command to kill innocent people, precisely because we recognize that duties and obligations do not give conclusive reasons for acting. And we regard his moral tone with contempt precisely because it seems inconceivable that a man should recognize certain moral claims on his action, while failing to recognize that these claims are overridden a thousandfold by other moral considerations.[7] Surely, we feel, he must have recognized that in this case he ought not to have done his duty, that the right course lay elsewhere.[b]

[b] There is a respect in which the account I have given here (of the force of judgments utilizing "ought" and "obligation") may seem paradoxical. As Joel Feinberg has pointed out to me, my account identifies one sense in which "ought" is "stronger" than "obligation" (since "ought-judgments" can be final, all-things-considered judgments), and another in which "ought" is "weaker" than "obligation" (since advice is "weaker" than requirement). For those who find this disturbing, it is worth emphasizing that "oughts" serve not only to give advice, but to identify justified behavior (as my discussion has suggested). The "must" of obligation holds its own against "normal" reasons people have for not wanting to discharge their obligations (e.g., reasons of convenience or personal

The significance of this discussion to an examination of political obligation should be clear. For to say of an individual that he has a political obligation (or a political duty) is not, on the view here expressed, to say that he ought to discharge the obligation, or that the obligation provides a conclusive reason for action. Political obligations (or duties) are only *one* sort of consideration relevant to a determination of how we ought to act within a political community. I will have more to say about this point in II.i and VIII.i.

I.ii. Obligation and Duty

Thus far we have treated the terms "obligation" and "duty" more or less indiscriminately. We have referred to the problem of political "obligation," but have also mentioned political "duty"; and we have distinguished other sorts of moral judgments from judgments of obligation and duty, as if "obligation" and "duty" could be used interchangeably. In fact, there is no denying the strong tendency in ordinary language to use these two terms interchangeably. But, on the other hand, we can identify clearly paradigmatic uses of these terms which reveal interesting differences, differences related to the different historical origins of the terms (as Richard Brandt has pointed out in a useful article).[8]

In this essay I will adopt, following Hart, Rawls, and others, uses of "obligation" and "duty" which are paradigmatic in Brandt's sense. But because I am adopting these specialized senses of the terms, it is important to

---

gain); and because of our desire for order and precision in our moral (and legal) lives, the requirements (and prohibitions) of obligation and duty are commonly expressed in exceptionless rules which ignore the complexity of special justifications (e.g., "Thou shalt not kill"). But this is in no way inconsistent with the recognition of moral (and legal) justifications for the performance of actions which are prohibited under "normal" circumstances.

note that in speaking of "the problem of political obligation," I will not be considering only those requirements
which are best called "obligations" (as opposed to
"duties"). For the problem of political obligation concerns moral requirements to act in certain ways in matters
political, and duties are just as much "moral requirements" as obligations. To presume that the moral bonds
in which we are interested are "obligations" (in our specialized sense), would appear to beg some important
questions. I will use "political obligation," therefore, as a
convenient shorthand for "political obligation or duty."
My adoption of the paradigmatic uses of "duty" and "obligation" is not, I should point out, simply an idle introduction of technical language; for although it involves
ignoring the looser or "extended" uses of these terms, the
terminology to be adopted distinguishes clearly and naturally between two types of moral requirements which
need to be distinguished in some way.

   Let us begin with "duty." It is clear from the start that
"duty" is used comfortably in two quite different sorts of
contexts. On the one hand, we commonly use the term
"duty" independent of any institutional setting or special
role which the duty-bound individual is supposed to be
playing. Thus, we may say, "It's our duty to go to the aid
of that drowning man." Here we refer to what is commonly called a "moral duty." On the other hand, we have
what I will call "positional duties" (I am not here assuming that the two types are mutually exclusive); these are
tasks or performances which are intimately connected
with some particular office, station, or role which an individual can fill. This role may be part of an institutional
framework, but it need not be. Thus, we speak of the
duties of a citizen, a teacher, or the president, but also of
the duties of a father. Positional duties can be referred to
even when no one has or has ever had those duties, for
they are tied to positions rather than to individuals. An
individual comes to have a positional duty only by filling
the position to which it is tied, and thereby coming to

have certain performances expected or required of him
within the scheme in question (be it institutional, familial, or whatever). When applying for a job, for instance,
we are told what our duties will be if we take the job, and
these duties can be called "the duties of an X," where "X"
is the name of the job in question. The term "responsibility" also seems to be particularly at home in such positional contexts, although it seems best reserved for required tasks which involve some independent planning
or nonroutine performance.[9] It should be noted that while
positional duties are requirements which must be met in
order to fill some position successfully, not *all* such requirements are duties.[10] The recent "sex scandals" in
Washington have shown that even for a politician there is
some behavior which is considered "unbecoming" to a
member of that profession; yet it is doubtful that among
the positional "duties" of a congressman is a duty not to
consort with prostitutes. Similarly, incompetence in a
congressman does not seem to be a shortcoming in terms
of duty, as, for instance, failing to appear in session or
misusing funds would be.

I will have more to say about "positional" or "institutional" duties, and their relation to moral requirements, in
I.iii. But in this essay we shall be chiefly concerned with
duties which are not tied to some role or position. These
duties are those which Rawls calls the "natural duties,"
and are moral requirements which apply to all men irrespective of status or of acts performed. Examples are the
duty to help those in need, the duty of justice (see Chapter
VI), and duties of nonmaleficence and respect.[11] These
duties are owed by all persons to all others and form the
core of what used to be known as "Natural Law." Those
uncomfortable with two types of duties ("positional" and
"natural") will no doubt observe that the natural duties
can be construed as "positional" by utilizing the "position" of "rational agent" or "creature capable of choice,"
etc. But I see little to be gained by such consolidation, and
it obscures the fact that the natural duties are moral re-

quirements, while a positional duty need be no more than the consequence of an established "requiring rule" in any institutional setting at all (see I.iii).

When we turn to "obligations," the paradigm case is quite different. Henceforth, when I speak of an "obligation," I will mean a moral requirement which satisfies the following four conditions (first specified by Hart).[12]

1. An obligation is a moral requirement generated by the performance of some voluntary act (or omission). This act may be a deliberate undertaking of an obligation, but it need not be. Unlike duties, then, obligations require special performances; this fact is reflected in language—we "obligate ourselves" but do not "duty ourselves." While we often come to have (positional) duties by voluntarily entering a position, we will normally then be in a position of having an *obligation* to perform the duties of that position.

2. An obligation is owed by a specific person (the "obligor") to a specific person or persons (the "obligee[s]"). Again, this distinguishes obligations from moral duties, which are owed by *all* persons to all others. And again language reflects this difference—while we "do" our duty, we "fulfill" or "discharge" an obligation; obligations are disposed of in a way that sounds very like the payment of a debt,[13] and this makes them seem more personal than duties. It should also be noted that obligations, being "dischargeable," can at least sometimes be disposed of once and for all, while moral duties remain always our duties.[c]

3. For every obligation generated, a correlative right is simultaneously generated. By incurring an obligation to do A, the obligor creates for the obligee a special right to the obligor's performance of A. Here I follow Hart, Feinberg, and others in accepting the logical correlativity of

[c] We do, of course, sometimes speak of "discharging" duties. Here I mean only to suggest that, e.g., by saving a drowning man I am not freed from my duty to help those in need, in the way that, by paying you what I owe you, I am freed from my obligation to repay my debt to you.

rights and obligations; the existence of an obligation entails the existence of a corresponding right. (As for the correlativity of rights and *duties*, see my remarks in Chapter VIII.) The language of rights provides another way of describing the distinction between obligations and natural duties. Obligations correlate with the "moral version" of what are called in legal jargon "rights in personam." These are rights which are held against a specific person, and are rights to a specific performance or forbearance (Hart calls these rights "special rights").[14] Duties, on the other hand, when they correlate with rights, correlate with "rights in rem," that is, rights which are held against all other people. And duties correlate with rights that are also held *by* all other people,[d] since if I have a duty to all men to refrain from stealing from them, all men have a right against me that I so refrain, as well as against everyone else (all this providing that the duty does correlate with a right). "In rem" rights are typically negative rights, rights to forbearances by all others. But there are positive "in rem" rights, such as the right to aid, which correlates with the duty to help those in need.[15]

4. It is the nature of the transaction or relationships into which the obligor and obligee enter, not the nature of the required act, which renders the act obligatory. While the fact that an act is morally impermissible may make it impossible for that act to be obligatory (consider the case of a promise to commit murder), an act's being morally acceptable or even praiseworthy cannot make the act *obligatory*. Obligations are not generated by the nature of the obligatory act.

These, then, are the features which distinguish obligations from duties. I will discuss in this essay four principles of obligation (which I believe to be *all* of the

[d] These are called by Hart "general rights" ("Are There Any Natural Rights?" pp. 187-188). General rights seem at first to be a proper subclass of "in rem" rights, being those "in rem" rights which all men possess. But it seems to me doubtful that there are any "in rem" rights which are *not* shared by all men.

principles of obligation): the principles of fidelity and consent, which account for what I will call "obligations of commitment"; and the principles of fair play and gratitude, which account for "obligations of reciprocation." The first two principles cover obligations deliberately undertaken (by promising or consenting), while the second two account for obligations generated by the receipt or acceptance of benefits. Only one natural duty, the natural duty of justice, will be discussed. I explain the apparent asymmetry in Chapter VI.

I.iii. Positional Duties and Moral Requirements

I have to this point touched only briefly on the distinction between "positional duties" and "moral duties" (or "natural duties"). But this distinction is an important one for any discussion of political obligation. For there are two sorts of positional duties which seem to be very closely related to political obligation, insofar as they are institutional requirements which concern obedience to law and citizenship. First, we have the "legal obligations" imposed by the legal system operative within the state. These "legal obligations" are positional duties attached to the position of "person within the domain of the state"; they are the legal requirements which must be met in order to avoid running afoul of the law and apply to all persons in the effective domain within which the legal system operates. Second, we have the so-called "duties of citizenship," positional duties attached to the position of "citizen" within some state. A citizen's "legal obligations" may be among these duties, as may be voting in elections, defending the country against invasion, reporting shirkers, and so on. It may well be that in many states the position of "citizen" is not taken seriously enough to warrant any serious talk of positional duties attached to that position. But clearly in many states there are performances which are expected or required within institutional frameworks better described as "political" than "legal."

The significance of these positional duties to an account of political obligation becomes apparent when we see that these positional duties may be believed to have *moral* weight, or indeed, to simply *be* moral requirements of a special sort. If this were true, the existence of "legal obligations" and "duties of citizenship" would establish certain moral constraints on the actions of all individuals within states with operative legal systems and on all individuals holding citizenship in states in which "duties of citizenship" were imposed. And these sorts of moral constraints would seem to be precisely what we are looking for in giving an account of political obligation.

I will argue that these positional duties do *not* have moral weight, that my (e.g.) "legal obligations" impose no *moral* constraints on my action. And, more generally, I will suggest that *no* positional duties establish anything concerning moral requirements. To see this, we must consider more carefully the significance of a "positional duty," in terms of the relations between "positional duties" and moral requirements (natural duties and obligations). To say of a man that he has a positional duty to do A, remember, is to say that because he occupies a certain position, role, or office within some established scheme or institution, he is required (or at least expected) by the scheme or institution to do A, as part of the "job" of a person in that position. Nonperformance of a positional duty may or may not make one vulnerable to coercive sanctions, but it will normally result in no less than strong disapproval from within the scheme. It must be remembered that to have a positional duty no *more* than this is necessary; for instance, it is not necessary that the scheme in question be useful or morally unobjectionable. So that while the President of the United States, the manager of the Yankees, and the dishwasher at Joe's all have positional duties, the Spanish Inquisitors, a leader of the Gestapo, and a member of the Ku Klux Klan all have positional duties in precisely the same sense. The positional duty to help exterminate the Jews and the positional duty to turn in the Yankee lineup card are on a par, as far as the relation between the act and the position is concerned. And this relation is all that need hold in order for an individual filling the position to have a positional duty to perform the act.

What, then, is the relation between these positional duties and moral requirements? In particular, does the existence of a positional duty to do A establish anything concerning a moral requirement to do A? It may seem at first that many positional duties simply *are* moral requirements, so that the existence of a positional duty is at some times sufficient to warrant the ascription of a moral requirement. Consider the following two cases. First, let us suppose that the holder of some great trust, say, the President of the United States, is guilty of grave failures in terms of doing "his duty as president"; the positional duties of his office, which set both limits and requirements, have not been performed. Do we not, in such a case, feel a *moral* outrage? Does it not seem that his positional duties were also *moral* duties? Second, consider the army medic who, with a tent full of wounded patients, wanders off to spend the afternoon in a Saigon bar. He has failed to perform his positional duties as an army medic, and will, it is hoped, answer for his failure. But are not these "military duties" also *moral* duties?

Both of these cases may appear to be instances where the existence of a positional duty is sufficient to establish a moral requirement (and, indeed, the positional duty seems identical to the moral requirement). But I believe that on closer examination we can see that this is not the case. Let us examine first the case of the president. Why do we feel that moral criticism is appropriate as a response to his shortcomings? This criticism is not justified, I suggest, simply because an officeholder has failed in his positional duties. For suppose that it were in the power of

Congress to appoint as president anyone they chose, and that tomorrow they chose *you*, forcing you to serve against your will. When you, overcome by frustration, weariness, and confusion, failed to perform the duties of your new office, would *you* be blameworthy in the same way? Clearly not, and the reason, I suggest, is that how the president got to *be* the president makes all the difference in evaluating his performance. The president is morally blameworthy because he voluntarily entered his position and undertook, in full knowledge of the details of the situation, to perform the duties of that position. When he failed in the job with which he had been entrusted, he violated an obligation which he had undertaken. And the source of our justified criticism is this failure to discharge an obligation (of great importance) to perform his positional duties. The mere failure to perform the duties does not, however, in the absence of such an obligation, necessarily justify criticism. And the existence of the positional duties is not sufficient to warrant the ascription of a moral requirement.

What, then, of our second example, the case of the army medic? The same analysis of this example seems possible, since he may have undertaken to perform the duties of a soldier. But let us suppose that he did not, that our army medic was inducted into the service against his will. It still seems as if in leaving the wounded to suffer and die he has failed not only to do his positional duty but to do his moral duty. And indeed he has, for he has a natural duty to help those in need where he can (with certain qualifications), a duty which is "nonpositional." In this case, the army medic has a moral duty to perform the same acts he has a positional duty to perform. But this former duty is not a duty "to perform his positional duties." For anyone, not just an army medic, has precisely the same duty to help those in need (although his medical skills make him better able to help). The duty here is completely independent of the position and the scheme or institution which defines it. The existence of the positional duty in no way establishes the moral requirement, but rather only happens to coincide with it. This independence from institutional roles, was, remember, one of the distinguishing features of a moral duty (I.ii) and explains why it is called a "natural" duty.

We have seen, then, two cases which at first seemed to be examples where the existence of a positional duty was sufficient to establish the existence of a moral requirement. But neither is in fact such an example. For in the first case, it was the manner in which the position was entered which established the moral requirement in question; an obligation to perform the positional duties was undertaken, and in the absence of this undertaking the fact that an individual had those positional duties established nothing. In the second case, the existence of the positional duty was irrelevant to the moral requirement, which anyone, regardless of position, would have in the situation described. There simply happened to be a natural duty to do what there was also a positional duty to do. I want to suggest, without going on endlessly examining examples, that all cases in which a positional duty seems to establish a moral requirement fit one of these two patterns, in which the *ground* of the moral requirement has nothing to do with the position, institution, or positional duties.

It is, of course, true that positional duties are at least *necessary* for us to have certain obligations, but only in a limited sense. Thus, I cannot undertake an obligation to perform the positional duties of an office unless that office and its duties exist. I can't promise and bind myself to, e.g., serve as a juror unless that position and the duties tied to it exist. There are, then (infinitely) many obligations we cannot have without positional duties. But these are not cases in which the existence of the positional duty is (or is part of) the *ground* of the moral requirement. The example mentioned is, for instance, one which falls under the principle of fidelity; our promises obligate us, but why this is so has nothing to do with the jury system or the duties of a juror.

This point is made by Michael Stocker, in his paper "Moral Duties, Institutions, and Natural Facts," by saying that positional duties (which he calls "institutional obligations") "play the same, or much the same, role vis-a-vis moral obligations as is played by such natural facts as someone's having typhoid":[16]

> For Smith to have a moral obligation to rid Jones of his typhoid, Jones must have typhoid. Nonetheless (Jones' having) typhoid is not morally relevant—except in regard to its effects, e.g., suffering and death. Typhoid itself, does not create, ground, or explain Smith's moral obligation, even though "typhoid" figures in its description and even though the obligation presupposes the existence of typhoid. Thus, the fact that a moral duty is described in a way (or is of a sort) that presupposes the existence of something— e.g., an institution—cannot be taken as showing that the institution, for example, creates, grounds, or explains the moral duty.[17]

The existence of a positional duty (i.e., someone's filling a position tied to certain duties) is a morally *neutral* fact. If a positional duty is binding on us, it is because there are grounds for a moral requirement to perform that positional duty which are independent of the position and the scheme which defines it. The existence of a positional duty, then, never establishes (by itself) a moral requirement. For to say of a man that he has a positional duty is merely to say that he is required by some scheme to do something related to the position he holds in that scheme; and this leaves both the nature of the scheme and the nature of the act required completely open.[18]

The importance of this position can be seen by comparing it with competing views, such as that developed in a recent paper by Haskell Fain:

> It is widely felt that . . . "de facto" institutional obligations are somehow less real, or less morally important, than those which can be morally rationalized according to some philosopher's pet moral theory. Now I do not believe that one can be morally indifferent to *any* of one's actual obligations—if one has a *military* obligation, for example, to obey one's superior officer, and soldiers do, then that obligation has *some* relative moral weight, however miniscule, in determining whether, say, a soldier should obey an order to shoot unarmed civilians.[19]

But surely Fain is mistaken here. Consider the case of an American civilian impressed into the British Navy during the eighteenth century. He has precisely the same "military obligations" (i.e., positional duties) as any other British seaman. But do these "military obligations" have *moral* weight? Surely not. He has no *obligations* to those who have forced him into a life of servitude, and his new positional duties do not seem to have any other sort of moral significance. He is no doubt "obliged" to obey, for British "military justice" has been renowned for centuries. But the suggestion that his new position in any way establishes *moral* constraints on his actions seems absurd. Perhaps we may be led to believe that soldiers' positional duties have moral weight by the belief that most soldiers serve voluntarily and undertake to perform their "military obligations." Even this latter belief seems false, but the important thing to note is that even in the case of the soldier who does serve voluntarily, it is not his "military obligations" which bind him, but rather the obligation which he has undertaken to discharge those positional duties. We must be careful, I am suggesting, always to distinguish the positional duty from the moral requirement; and I have urged that the former never be thought to ground the latter, or indeed, to have any moral weight at all.

These conclusions apply, of course, to the positional duties which we considered earlier—"legal obligations" and the "duties of citizenship." If my argument has been sound, the fact that I have a "legal obligation" or a "duty of citizenship" will be a morally *neutral* fact; nothing will follow from this fact about any moral constraints on my actions. We will want here to distinguish between "the obligation to obey the law," which is a *moral* requirement, and our "legal obligations," which are not. To speak of our "legal obligations" is only to use a convenient shorthand for referring to the set of requiring rules imposed by our legal system, and the mere existence of such a set of rules is never, in itself, sufficient to establish any moral requirement. Similarly, we can distinguish between our "political obligations" and our "duties of citizenship." In both cases, the distinction is between a moral requirement to fulfill positional duties and the positional duties themselves.[20]

If I am right, then, we cannot produce an account of political obligation (or of the obligation to obey the law) which relies solely on the existence of certain positional duties. The mere fact that an institution (or set of institutions) exists, and that its rules apply to me, will not bind me to that institution. If I am morally bound to obey the law or to be a good citizen, the ground of this bond will be independent of the legal and political institutions in question (in the sense that their mere existence does not constitute a ground). And this seems to be as it should, for certainly we do not feel that perverse legal systems or tyrannical governments deserve our support; yet they are not "unreal" for this reason, nor do they fail to impose positional duties on those unhappy persons subject to them. We will look, then, for the ground of political obligation not in the existence of certain sorts of institutions, but rather in moral principles which are "natural" or "noninstitutional."

I.iv. "Prima Facie" Requirements

One possible response to the line of reasoning sketched above utilizes the notion of a "prima facie" obligation. Positional duties are not, this response admits, genuine moral duties or obligations, nor do they necessarily ground such moral requirements. But this is not to say that they have no moral weight at all. Positional duties are "prima facie" moral requirements.[21] Thus, our "legal obligations," for instance, sometimes do not impose any moral constraints on our action; when there are strong reasons for disobedience, these "prima facie" obligations have no weight. But in the absence of such reasons, our "legal obligations" bind us, for what was only a "prima facie" moral consideration then becomes "actual." All positional duties, then, are "prima facie" obligatory.

In order to understand and respond to this line of argument, we will have to get clear about the force of the "prima facie-actual" distinction at work in it. The terminology originates, of course, in Ross. Most of the uses of the distinction since that time have had a curious "sleight-of-hand" look about them, perhaps because it is so difficult to pin down the content of the original Rossian distinction. As Ross explains the distinction, the difference between actual and prima facie duties is best expressed in terms of the difference between something's really being our duty and only "tending to be" our duty. Prima facie duties "are not strictly speaking duties, but things that tend to be our duty. . . ."[22] So while a prima facie duty is not, for Ross, really a duty, it is "something related in a special way to duty."[23]

In order to understand these explanations, we must try to understand Ross's motives for introducing the distinction. Ross saw quite clearly that moral claims are often legitimately overridden. In particular, he was concerned with the sort of case in which I am justified in breaking a promise to meet a friend for lunch, say, in order to prevent great suffering or death by aiding the victim of an accident. My promise certainly establishes a moral claim on my action, yet there is little doubt that morality requires nonfulfillment of my promise in such a case. How are we to explain the resolution of this direct conflict of moral claims on my action? Ross was (rightly) dissatisfied with the (partial) Kantian solution of "ranking" duties as "perfect" and "imperfect." But at the same time it seemed to him improper to classify both moral claims as genuine duties (in the full sense), for (in Ross) to act morally is simply "to do your duty." How, then, could the promise in our example generate a duty, when in order to act morally I must *break* the promise? Ross's answer is that my promise generates only a "prima facie" duty, something which "tends to be" my duty. But my "actual" duty consists in aiding the accident victim.

Unhappily for Ross's solution, there is a perfectly natural way of handling these "conflicts of duty," without resorting to his peculiar "tendency to be right (or required)." Once we understand that duties (and obligations) do not exhaust the subject matter of morality, we will have no difficulty accepting that we sometimes have duties which we ought not to fulfill. Ross's problem ceases to be a problem. Duties which conflict or are overridden are genuine duties, not "tendencies to be duties." This fact can perhaps be seen most clearly by noting that even when they conflict or are overridden, duties and obligations continue to have moral weight, to be matters to consider seriously. Surprisingly, perhaps, Ross sees this quite clearly.[24] And that may incline us to believe that Ross is not really denying that prima facie duties are genuine moral requirements, after all. If not, then perhaps my objections to Ross's distinction are only in fact objections to his way of characterizing it. Certainly, however, such objections are justified. For Ross's terminology forces us into an uncomfortable *reversal* of the uses of the terms in question.[25] Where we would normally speak of an "obligation," as when a promise has been made, Ross would have us speak of a "prima facie obligation," which is "strictly speaking" not an obligation at all. And where we want to speak of "what we ought to do, all things considered," Ross would have us speak of an (actual) obligation!

There are, of course, other well-known objections to the Rossian distinction;[26] I will not belabor the point any further here. For we can already see that the argument with which we began—namely, that positional duties are "prima facie" moral requirements—cannot succeed. *All* moral requirements are "prima facie" in one sense and "actual" in another. They are "prima facie" in the sense that they do not provide conclusive reasons for action, and "actual" in the sense that they are not "tendencies to be requirements" or "probable requirements." But *no* moral requirements are "prima facie" in the sense required by the argument in question; *no* moral requirements are only *sometimes* morally weighty (i.e., when they change status from "prima facie" to "actual"). My "legal obligations," for instance, are either moral requirements or not. There is no "prima facie" middle ground. But I have already argued that no positional duty is a moral requirement, from which it follows that my "legal obligations" are not moral requirements at all. No specialized "prima facie" jargon will allow us to avoid that conclusion.

There is, of course, a revised version of the prima facie-actual distinction which can be seen in the work of many contemporary philosophers. And we often read that political obligations or the obligation to obey the law are only "prima facie" obligations in this revised sense. According to the revised account, both prima facie and actual obligations are genuine obligations. But a prima facie obligation is now an obligation considered from a "limited point of view," that is, one which provides a reason for action which may be overridden; an actual obligation, on the other hand, is "an obligation, all things considered," and provides a conclusive reason for action. This account, or something like it, seems to be accepted by many philosophers.[27]

But I would like to urge that the prima facie-actual terminology be avoided altogether, for a number of reasons. First, it should be obvious that the distinction as outlined above corresponds to the distinction discussed in I.i between obligations and "what we ought to do, all things considered." We already have, then, a perfectly natural way to speak of the distinction, one which corresponds closely to ordinary language; the special jargon fills no linguistic void.[e] And the prima facie-actual language, rather than clarifying any problems in moral philosophy, seems only to generate results which are counterintuitive. Thus, an obligation can change status or "mode" while "all things are being considered," changing from a prima facie to an actual obligation during the consideration of evidence. This result alone seems sufficiently peculiar to warrant rejection of the prima facie-actual terminology.

The most objectionable consequence of using any version of the prima facie-actual distinction, however, is that it tends to obscure the differences between two sorts of reasons which are important in moral matters,[28] to the point where one forgets that when a "prima facie" obligation is overridden, it is a real obligation which continues to have moral weight even while being overridden.[f] When obligations are overridden and rights infringed, they do

[e] This is not to say that ordinary moral language does not in some ways support the prima facie-actual distinction. It is not uncommon to hear people ask, "But which of these duties is really my duty?" Such language immediately suggests the Rossian distinction. But for reasons elaborated below, the distinction should nonetheless be rejected.

[f] Consider here the parallel with reasons. It is a common mistake to suppose that a reason is not really a reason unless it is a weighty or even conclusive reason. When I tell my wife that my reason for wanting to buy a car is that I like the design of its glove compartment, she may respond, "That's no reason!" But the fact remains that it is a reason, even though it has comparatively little weight. And when it is overridden by better reasons not to buy the car, it does not cease to be a reason for buying it.

not "fade away" in the interest of the "actual obligation," they are not simply to be forgotten. The fact that I have an obligation may call for special behavior on my part, even where I do not and ought not to discharge it. By modifying the language of obligation with "prima facie" and "actual," we tend to obscure these facts. Perhaps the "legal" sense of "prima facie" is partly to blame here, for "prima facie" is used in legal contexts to label, for instance, evidence or testimony which requires refutation; but once refuted, it ceases to be of any importance. Obligations, however, do not cease to be important simply because overridden. At best, the revised prima facie-actual distinction seems to me to have little clarificatory value, while at worst it can promote harmful misunderstanding. For that reason it is best discarded.

The slate is not wiped clean. Similarly, overriding moral considerations do not wipe the "moral slate" clean of overridden obligations and infringed rights. Herbert Morris may have a similar point in mind, in "Persons and Punishments," *Monist* 52 (October 1968).

CHAPTER II

The Problem of
Political Obligation

II.i. The Limits of the Investigation

With our preliminary account of obligations and institutional requirements complete, it is possible to turn our full attention to the problem of political obligation. We have seen that (as a rough approximation) a political obligation is a moral requirement to support and comply with the political institutions of one's country of residence. Before we can be more specific, however, it is still important that we determine what a complete account of political obligation can be reasonably ·expected to provide, and what conditions will have to be satisfied if it is to count as a successful account. We must, in other words, specify the goals to strive toward. These matters will be, in part, the subject of the present chapter. I will also consider here two approaches to the problem of political obligation which I wish to reject from the start. But my primary purpose will be to establish the limits of my investigation, in preparation for advancing to the main lines of argument in Chapter III.

I want now to make four suggestions concerning what we want when we ask for an account of political obligation. Given the confusion surrounding this topic, I take this initial task to be very important. I am not familiar with any discussions of political obligation which agree with me on all four counts. Still, we can hardly regard these suggestions as flying in the face of tradition, for there appears to be no coherent tradition to challenge.

1. Perhaps the most common misconception about a theory of political obligation is that it has far more immediate practical consequences than it does in fact have.

In specifying our political obligations, we do not answer the question "how ought we to act, all things considered, in matters political?", or even the more limited question "ought we to obey the law?" The discussion of the differences between judgments of obligation and judgments of what we ought to do (I.i) should have made this quite clear. Our political obligations will certainly be a consideration, and usually a very important one, in any determination of how we ought to act within a political community. But a conclusion about these obligations alone will not *be* a determination of how we ought to act all things considered. A number of other factors typically enter into such a determination, such as duties we have toward particular persons qua persons (as opposed to "qua citizens"), as well as duties of a specifically political nature (if there are such) which do not properly fall within the class of moral requirements in which we are interested (see section 2 below for a clarification of this point).

As a result, the potential revolutionary or conscientious objector should not look for a theory of political obligation to yield final conclusions as to how he ought to act; rather, he should expect such a theory only to aid him in his understanding of one sort of obligation which should be considered prior to any decision. I will not, therefore, deal here with the problems of revolution and disobedience to law, beyond making the simple observation that neither a conclusion that we are all bound by political obligations nor a conclusion that no one is so bound will be decisive in a justification of revolution or disobedience (although it would certainly be important to one). In this I depart significantly from the majority of writers on the subject of political obligation, who have seen a much stronger connection between a theory of political obligation and a justification of revolution or disobedience.[1]

2. What precisely are the sorts of moral requirements in which a theory of political obligation is interested? I have already suggested that in referring to political *obligation*, I do not mean to narrow our field of possible answers only

to those moral requirements best described as obligations;
a duty, for instance, might be the bond in which we are
interested. But I do want to suggest that we are only interested in those moral requirements which bind an individual to one *particular* political community, set of political
institutions, etc. This suggestion should not be surprising
in light of my previous remarks on the connection between the notions of political obligation and citizenship.
And yet, while it may seem innocuous on the surface, this
"particularity requirement," as I shall call it, will exclude
many traditional attempts to answer questions about
political obligation.

Consider, for instance, the suggestions that our political
obligations consist in our being bound to support or comply with: governments in power, just governments, beneficial governments, etc. Each of these bonds would be
relevant to any determination of how we ought to act in
matters political, but none would be a political obligation
in the right sense, for none of the principles under which
these bonds fall is "particularized." By this I mean that
under these principles an individual may be bound by
one moral bond to many different governments. Let me
explain what may seem a counterintuitive suggestion
with an example. The motivation for the "particularity requirement" will then become more apparent.

Suppose we accepted one of the suggestions listed
above, say, that we have an obligation or a duty to support
just governments, and that this is what our political obligation consists in. And suppose that I am a citizen living
under a just government. While it follows that I have an
obligation to support my government, it does not follow
that there is anything *special* about this obligation. I am
equally constrained by the same moral bond to support
every other just government. Thus, the obligation in question would not bind me to any particular political authority in the way we want. If political obligation and citizenship are to be related as I have suggested they should be,
we need a principle of political obligation which binds

the citizen to one *particular* state above all others, namely that state in which he is a citizen.[g] And none of the suggestions considered above will meet this "particularity requirement." For that reason, this requirement rules out not only these suggestions, but many other traditional but "nonparticularized" principles which have been offered as answers to questions about political obligation.

It is a commonplace, however, for those who advance such nonparticularized principles to *assume* a particularized application. Thus, in saying that we are bound to support just governments, we might take this to mean that we are bound to our own just governments, and to no others. But we cannot allow this slide without asking why a government's being *ours* should be significant in this way. And the answer to that question may of necessity refer to features of the citizen-state relationship which are *themselves* grounds of a moral requirement falling under a particularized principle of a quite different sort (e.g., a principle of consent or fair play); but in that case, the general principle in question, namely that we ought to support just governments, looks expendable. All of the moral work seems to be done by those features of the citizen-state relationship which make a government's being ours morally significant. It may be quite illegitimate, then, merely to *assume* a particularized application of a principle of obligation in this way. The sort of argument sketched above will be filled out in Chapter VI.

Now, it might be answered that we could legitimately particularize a principle of political obligation in one way that would not bring in new morally significant features of the citizen-state relationship as suggested above. We

---

[g] The problem becomes particularly apparent if we imagine that I am living under an unjust government in a country at war with another, justly governed, country. Could we seriously maintain that my "political obligation" consists in *opposing* the efforts of my own country, in favor of a country with which I may have no significant relations whatever. While we may believe that I have a duty to oppose my country, this is surely ill-described as my "political obligation."

might hold that mere physical proximity is sufficient to make a nonparticularized obligation particular in the sense I require. In other words, simply because I am living within the domain of just government A, a principle which binds us to support just governments binds me to government A and to no other just government. This sort of argument seems to be lurking behind the presentation of many nonparticularized principles (e.g., see my discussion of Rawls's "Natural Duty of Justice" in Chapter VI). But why should we accept this argument? Living in the domain of government A certainly makes it *easier* for me to support government A than to support any other just government; but it is not obvious that this should affect the scope of the moral requirement to support just governments. If we allowed such a move, it would follow that when I go to live for a month with my friends in the domain of just government B, all of my political obligations would transfer automatically to government B, regardless of whether I have any other significant relations with that government. But this seems wildly implausible, unless we believe that my residence in this domain *in itself* establishes for me an obligation to support government B (as it would, say, using the Lockean conception of "tacit consent through residence"). I hope to show that such beliefs are unfounded. Here, however, the point to note is that even if my residence in the domain of just government B *were* morally significant in this way, the moral bond generated would be a new "particularized" bond, quite unrelated to any duty or obligation I might have to support just governments. We cannot, then, accept the suggestion that mere physical proximity "particularizes" the sorts of moral bonds we have been considering. Such an argument breaks down the relationship we want between political obligation and citizenship. Only if we are willing to accept that our political obligations can transfer from government to government as we travel the world, will this suggestion seem even prima facie attractive. But even if we are willing to accept such a consequence, it would seem to be residence itself, and not the quality (e.g., the justice) of the governments involved, which grounds the moral bonds in question. Most of us do not, of course, regard mere residence as significant in this way, for we do not believe the political obligations of citizens to be identical to the obligations of visiting aliens.[h]

I stand firm, then, in requiring "particularity" in answers to questions about political obligation. The sorts of principles of obligation in which we will be interested will for that reason characteristically mention special relationships with the state into which an individual can enter (e.g., by promising, consenting, accepting or receiving benefits, etc.). It is these special relationships which bind the individual to one particular set of political institutions, political community, etc. While particularized principles of this sort do leave open the possibility of conflicting obligations (e.g., when an individual contracts with two different governments), each of these obligations still binds the individual to only one state. The proper relationship between the political obligation and citizenship is thus preserved. But it is not preserved in the case of a nonparticularized bond which ties us to more than one government. The particularity requirement, as I have stated it, is set out nowhere in the literature with which I am familiar; but in their concern with "special relationships" between citizen and state, the classical works in

[h] This again seems clearest in the event of war, where visiting aliens are not supposed by anyone to be bound to participate in the country's military efforts. In fact, this intuition is given voice in the principle of international law which specifies that aliens have no specifically "political" duties toward their host countries, but are bound only to conform to the "social order" of those countries. See Michael Walzer's discussion in *Obligations: Essays on Disobedience, War, and Citizenship*, Simon and Schuster, 1971, p. 103. A. C. Ewing makes a similar point: "that we have some special obligation to our country is a view not confined to rabid nationalists but almost universally held. This appears particularly clearly in the case of war" (*The Individual, the State, and World Government*, Macmillan, 1947, p. 213).

political theory nearly all display a concern to meet some (unstated) requirement of particularity.

3. Though I want to require particularity, I want to deny the need for two other limits which are often laid down for a theory of political obligation. The first of these is the requirement of singularity in ground. Essentially this is the requirement that there be one and only one ground of political obligation. Perhaps the consent theorists have been more guilty of this mistake than anyone else (although they have, at least, allowed various kinds of consent as possible grounds). But other sorts of political philosophers have narrowed their sights in a similar fashion.[2] That this is a mistake is, I assume, fairly obvious; a *presumption* in favor of singularity seems, in the absence of special argument, unwarranted. We might note in this context that even the first recorded argument for political obligation, that of Socrates in Plato's *Crito*, suggested at least three distinct grounds of political obligation (that the state was a good state and was thus owed obedience, that the state was a benefactor to be repaid, and that Socrates had tacitly consented to the state's authority over him and so become bound).[3]

4. A more frequently made mistake is that of demanding the "universality" of political obligations over some range of persons (e.g., over all men, over all citizens of a particular state, etc.). It is often assumed that if we cannot give an account of political obligation which shows that everyone in, e.g., a particular state is bound, then we cannot give an account of political obligation which applies to anyone in that state. John Ladd, for instance, insists that political obligation must be a single "universal moral requirement binding on everyone in the society";[4] this specification combines both the demand for singularity in ground and the demand for universality (and is, as a result, "doubly damned" in my view).

More frequently, of course, political philosophers have required only "universality," not combining this with the

demand for "singularity in ground." There are many contemporary examples of such a requirement,[5] but perhaps
Joseph Tussman's efforts to "obligate" the entire body
politic is the best example in recent years of tailoring a
theory of political obligation to meet this confused requirement.[6] The demand common to these writers is that
political obligation be what M.B.E. Smith has called a
"generic obligation";[i] the obligation is supposed to be one
which all citizens, or else all citizens in some particular
state, owe to their government. If the obligation is not
"generic" in this sense, then it must be a fiction.

I suggest that this "all-or-nothing" attitude is confused
primarily because I can see no obvious objections to a
theory which allows that some people have political obligations while others, and even others in the same state, do
not. A theory of political obligation ought to tell us what
class of people are bound to their governments, and why;
if it tells us that only certain people are so bound, people
who have, say, performed some special act, the theory is
not obviously defective because it tells us this. Now we
might, of course, believe that no government is legitimate
to which *every* citizen is not obligated, and that *no* citizen
can be obligated to an illegitimate government. The demand for "universality" within good governments might

---

[i] M.B.E. Smith, "Is There a Prima Facie Obligation to Obey the Law?",
Yale Law Journal 82 (1973). Smith calls "generic" an obligation shared
by all persons who meet a certain description. Apparently, he realizes
that *any* obligation is "generic" on this definition, but finds the distinction useful in spite of this. The real force of the distinction, I think, is
supposed to be that a "generic obligation" is one necessarily shared by
all members of some group (more than one person), that group not being
defined by reference to some acknowledged principle of obligation (e.g.,
the group of people who have made binding promises would not be the
right sort of group). Examples of generic obligations might be the obligations parents have to care for their children, or doctors to care for their
patients, or politicians to act in the interest of their constituents or countries. If there are such obligations, none of the relevant groups is defined
in reference to the principle of obligation under which the group members are bound. Smith does not say that this is what he means by
"generic obligation," but it is, I think, a useful concept only if so defined.

then be understandable, for if even one citizen were not politically bound, the government would be illegitimate and hence no one would be so bound. But the belief on which this supposed need for the universality requirement is based is false.[7] It might also be disquieting if, in a case where only some citizens of a particular state were politically bound, we were forced to conclude from this that the government could only justifiably coerce a certain segment of the people living within its domain. But in the first place, it is not obvious that such a conclusion follows. Second, however, the fact that such a conclusion would be disturbing is not obviously a good reason for rejecting the theory that leads us to it. In the absence of argument, then, I will not presume the need for "universality." Finally, a good practical reason for not demanding universality is that with this demand in mind, the theorist too easily finds grounds of obligation where there are none, believing that he must account for everyone or despair of accounting for anyone. The notorious Lockean "tacit consent" which consists only in residence, and the "child's obligations" of Tussman's uneducated citizens are cases in point.

Let me summarize the results of this section briefly. First, in asking for an account of political obligation, we are not asking for an account of what individuals ought to do, all things considered, within their communities. Nor are we asking only about the moral bonds these individuals may have which are best described as "obligations"; "duties" may figure in our discussion as well. Second, we are interested only in those moral bonds which bind individuals to *particular* political communities or governments, as opposed to "types" of communities or governments. Finally, we are interested not in choosing a single ground of obligation or duty, or one which applies to all members of a given group, but rather in describing all moral requirements which bind citizens to their political communities. I hope that by setting out these guidelines I will have sufficiently alerted the reader to the fact that I am dealing in this essay with a very special sense of "political obligation," one which I do not claim to be widely accepted by political philosophers. What I do claim for the notion of political obligation described in this section is that it captures the spirit of the classical treatises on political obligation and takes seriously the idea that political obligation is a special kind of obligation.

II.ii. Political Obligation and Political Language

I have suggested that we should not simply presume that either everyone or no one in a state has political obligations. But it is certainly true that, on a purely intuitive level, we do believe that at least most citizens are in some way bound to support and comply with their political authorities (at least in reasonably just states). If we cannot, then, develop a plausible account of political obligation which is at least reasonably general in its application, we must presumably draw one of three conclusions. Either: 1) substantive moral assumptions on this subject have been mistaken (being a product, say, of early political inculcation), 2) our examination of the possibilities was incomplete, or 3) our basic conception of our project was in error. I want briefly to consider this last conclusion.

It has at various times, at least in this century, been fashionable on several fronts to suggest that when we ask whether or why people are obligated to obey the law or support legitimate governments, we are in some basic way showing our misunderstanding of political life or political concepts. One such front stems from the neo-Hegelian political theory of T. H. Green, as developed in his well-known *Lectures on the Principles of Political Obligation*.[8] Green, of course, approached the problem of political obligation in a very different way than I shall in this essay, and it would not pay us, I believe, to try to reconstruct and criticize the arguments; I instead direct the reader to H. A. Prichard's sometimes illuminating essay on Green's *Lectures*.[9] On another related front, various charges have been made that traditional approaches to political obligation tend to "moralize" politics in an objectionable way.[10] But a more interesting argument, one that I will deal with in some detail, stems from what might be called the "linguistic front"; it has been defended by Hanna Pitkin in her paper "Obligation and Consent," and in the works of several other writers on the subject.[11]

This argument is supposed to show us that questions like "Why are we obligated to obey the government (the law, political authorities, etc.)?" are symptomatic of a "conceptual confusion." Terms like "authority," "law," and "government" are grammatically or conceptually tied to "obligation," in the same way that "promise" is.[12] It simply follows from our calling something a "legitimate government" that we have an obligation to obey and support it. As Pitkin puts it:

> Now the same line of reasoning can be applied to the question "why does even a legitimate government, a valid law, a genuine authority ever obligate me to obey?" As with promises . . . we may say that this is what "legitimate government," "valid law," "genuine authority" mean. It is part of the concept, the meaning of "authority," that those subject to it are required to obey, that it has a right to command. It is part of the concept, the meaning of "law," that those to whom it is applicable are obligated to obey it. As with promises, so with authority, government, and law: there is a prima facie obligation involved in each, and normally you must perform it.[13]

We are given three expressions here, each of which is supposed to "involve" conceptually an obligation to obey: "valid law," "genuine authority," "legitimate government." We may, I think, dispose of the first suggestion fairly quickly; for certainly we do *not* normally mean by

"valid law" a "law which we have an obligation to obey,"
nor is any such obligation implied in calling a law valid.
In calling a law valid, we normally mean only that it
originated at an appropriate law-giving source. And while
we might, if we were natural law theorists, insist that only
good laws which we are obligated to obey are valid laws,
or that only laws created by, e.g., a representative body are
valid, these are specialized, theory-dependent senses of
"valid law." Pitkin gives us no reason to suppose that one
of these special senses is what she has in mind. If it is not,
then we can perhaps attribute her claim to a confusion between "legal obligations" (which are tied to "valid law"
in the way she suggests) and the "obligation to obey the
law" (which is not). But only the latter, of course, would
serve Pitkin's purposes here. I have dealt with this confusion already (in I.iii), so we need not belabor the point
here.

"Genuine authority" and "legitimate government" are
somewhat more difficult to deal with, simply because they
are more obscure expressions than "valid law." But since
I suspect that Pitkin means by "valid law" precisely "law
originating from a legitimate government with genuine
authority," we will probably be aided in understanding
her claims concerning the expression "valid law" by
analyzing her claim that the expressions "legitimate government" and "genuine authority" are conceptually tied
to the obligation to obey. Now, an obvious sort of reply to
this claim is to point out that by "legitimate government,"
for instance, we may mean many very different things.
Sometimes in calling a government legitimate we mean
that it has acquired its political power in the proper way
(e.g., by free election rather than by military overthrow or
conquest), regardless of the quality of the government.
Sometimes we call a government legitimate if it is a good
government, regardless of how it obtained its power; thus,
we may hold that a government is legitimate if and only if
it serves the interests of its citizens, does so fairly and in
accordance with their wishes, remains open to change,

etc. (all within reasonable limits). In a different sort of context, such as an international one, we may call a government legitimate if it is recognized as legitimate by other governments, or if it exercises effective control over a certain population. And just as often as any of these, we will mean by "legitimate government" a government which meets some combination of these various purported criteria.

So it clearly will not do to tell us simply that part of the meaning of "legitimate government" is "government we are obligated to obey." But suppose we allow that by "legitimate government" Pitkin means a government which satisfies *all* of these conditions for legitimacy. Will it then be true that the existence of a legitimate government "entails" the existence of an obligation to obey it, as Pitkin claims? Surely, even in that case, there will be something more to consider; for Pitkin does not want to suggest that everyone everywhere has an obligation to obey this legitimate government (and on this point, remember our discussion of the "particularity requirement" in II.i). The conclusion that Pitkin seems to want is that from the existence of a legitimate government it follows that all those persons over whom that government has "genuine authority" are obligated to obey it. So now we have arrived at still another obscure expression in need of analysis.

And clearly, there are as many senses of "having authority" as there were of "legitimacy." But let us again examine the sense most favorable to Pitkin's argument. We will disregard the so-called "de facto" notions of authority, and "conventional authority," since it is clearly doubtful that any obligations follow from these sorts of authority.[14] The government's claims to authority, the claims it makes which are recognized by other governments, and the government's actual power to coerce all seem quite insufficient to establish any conclusions concerning a citizen's obligation to obey. We should consider instead some "de jure" notion of authority which involves having a right to command and be obeyed. Is it true, then, that "legitimate government" means, at least in part, "government which all persons over whom the government has genuine (de jure) authority are obligated to obey"?

If we granted Pitkin this point, what would we have granted? Surely we would still want to ask how and over whom a government comes to have this sort of authority. And if we explain, as seems natural, that this authority is gotten by being granted by citizens, say, or by the government's having extended certain benefits to its citizens, we have come not just to an explanation of this political authority, but to a *ground* of the political obligation in question. And for that reason, it no longer looks as if we are confused when we ask "Why are we obligated to obey this legitimate government with genuine authority?" The answer to the question is not "because that's what 'legitimate government with genuine authority' means." There is a simple answer, and it refers to the ground of the obligation in question—for example, "you are obligated because you've done X," where 'X' may be "accepted certain benefits," or "contracted with the government," etc. When we ask what Pitkin takes to be the confused question, we are asking for the *ground* of our political obligation; and this is symptomatic of no conceptual difficulties.

A parallel example may help to make my point clearer.[15] Let us suppose, as seems likely, that it is analytic that magnets attract iron, that "object which attracts iron" is at least part of the meaning of "magnet." Still, the question "Why do magnets attract iron?" is not a confused question, or one to which we would answer "because that's what 'magnet' means." Rather, it is a question which asks for an *explanation* of a magnet's attraction for iron, and this explanation is by no means required only by the confused or weak of mind. Similarly, even if Pitkin is right that "we are obligated to obey legitimate governments with genuine authority" is analytic, it does *not* follow that in asking *why* this is so we are betraying our confusion about political concepts. For once again we are not asking to be reminded of meanings; instead, we are asking for an explanation, in the form of the *ground* of this obligation.

But it might be objected that Pitkin's point goes much deeper than I have made it seem. For in talking of legitimacy and authority, Pitkin (with most of the others who present such arguments) has really been trying to focus our attention on the moral quality of governments, and the role that this quality plays in the generation of political obligations. The point is not just that certain traditional questions about political obligation are confused, but that traditional political theorists tend to look to the wrong sorts of things in trying to understand political obligation. They tend to look at specific acts that individuals perform, at benefits they receive, and, in general, at individuals' political lives. But this is to get started on the wrong foot; the political theorist ought to look instead, the argument goes, to the quality of the government in question. For from the fact that a government is a good one (in various ways), political obligations follow for citizens living under it, quite independent of their individual histories. A good government is simply one which we have an obligation to obey, regardless of our individual histories. And while this may not be an analytic truth, as Pitkin wants it to be, it has not been shown to be false.

Now there are several difficulties with this line of argument. First, there are difficulties which revolve around the "particularity requirement" specified in II.ii. We do not want an account of political obligation which binds us to all good governments equally. But when we try to "particularize" this obligation in the right way, new difficulties emerge. For such a particularization requires us to say that we have an obligation to support and obey a good government only if, say, we live within its domain, or if it "applies" to us.[16]

But beyond these considerations, there are other obstacles to the view under examination, i.e., the view that we ought to focus on the quality of government rather than on individuals' political histories in analyzing political obligation. Specifically, it seems to me odd to suggest that we can locate and discuss something called "the quality of the government" which is completely divorced from the actual effects of government action on individual citizens, and then argue from this "quality" to the obligations those citizens have to obey the government. The only sort of "quality of government" that seems relevant here is the quality that is transmitted to actual persons. Thus, good governments are those which, among other things, extend the benefits of government in large doses to those living under them. There is a sense, then, in which we must refer to individual histories in order to determine the quality of government. It becomes paradoxical, therefore, to demand that we look to the quality of the government *rather than to* individual histories.

But it might be replied that we are taking the demand too literally. Really what the demand boils down to is that, for instance, in the case of a particular citizen within a state with a good government who does not, e.g., receive any of the benefits of government, we should look first to the fact that he lives under a good government. Rather than saying "there is nothing in his individual political history which binds him," we should say "he lives under a good government, so he is bound." But certainly this is a very peculiar and apparently unwarranted claim. The claim that a man who has neither given his consent to nor received benefits from a government may be bound to it nonetheless by the unhappy accident of living within its recognized domain, certainly requires a good deal of argument to support it.

I think, then, that there are strong reasons for rejecting this whole suggested way of approaching the problem of political obligation. In what follows, I will utilize the more traditional approach, concentrating on individuals' political histories and analyzing their obligations in terms of acts performed, benefits received, etc. The considerations raised in this chapter seem to me to show this sort of approach to be the correct one.

What I have called the traditional approach is commonly characterized as deontological and "backward looking." It finds the grounds of obligations in past (or continuing) performances or events, such as consenting or benefaction. By contrast, utilitarianism (and similar teleological theories) are often described as "forward looking." We can, very loosely, class as utilitarian any theory which holds that the only acts (or kinds of acts) which are morally right are those which promote (or tend to promote) "social utility" or "the general happiness." (At least since Sidgwick it has been common to substitute "maximize" for "promote" in this rough definition.) Insofar as we have obligations on a simple utilitarian theory, then, these are grounded not in past performances or events, but in the probable future consequences of our actions. The determination of our moral bonds is thus "forward looking" (though this is only obviously true of some forms of utilitarianism). Because a utilitarian approach to the problem of political obligation contrasts in this way with the traditional approach, it is important to evaluate utilitarianism's account before proceeding.

II.iii. Utilitarianism and Political Obligation

Utilitarianism continues to survive as an attractive and widely supported moral theory, despite constant assault by devoted deontologists. Even those who advocate competing theories acknowledge, by their arguments, that utilitarianism is an option still to be taken seriously. In the face of justified suspicions about the authority of the "Morality of Common Sense" (to use Sidgwick's phrase), "standard" counterexamples to utilitarianism seem less than overwhelming. As a result, any serious approach to the problem of political obligation must consider the possibility of giving a utilitarian account of our political bonds.

My object, in the very brief discussion of utilitarianism to follow, will not be to weigh the merits of that theory as a whole; I will not ask whether the principle of utility is a (or the) valid moral principle. Instead, I will ask only whether utilitarianism, in its plausible form(s), could yield an account of political obligation of the sort we want. To answer this question, one need not decide the broader and more difficult issue. And because I hope to show that utilitarianism cannot provide an account of political obligation (in the strict sense of the phrase, specified above), we should be able to avoid the general problem of justification altogether at this point. I want to stress here that my criticism of possible (and attempted) utilitarian accounts of political obligation is not to be taken as a criticism of utilitarianism. If there were no widespread political obligations, utilitarianism could not be faulted for its inability to account for such obligations; and we have not yet decided that all, most, or any of us have political obligations. Whether the argument of this section gives us reason to reject utilitarianism, then, must depend on the ultimate outcome of our investigation. My procedure will be similar in the chapters which follow: I will try first to put the principles in question in their most defensible forms, asking whether, so understood, they can provide an account of political obligation. Only after doing so will I consider, where necessary, broader questions of justification.

Examples of utilitarian accounts of political obligation are not easy to find among the writings of the classical utilitarians. Hume, of course, sketched a (broadly) utilitarian theory of allegiance in both *A Treatise of Human Nature* (Book III, Part II) and his essay "Of the Original Contract." Neither Bentham nor Mill, however, followed with an improved or more explicit account, and neither demonstrated any concern over possible difficulties with Hume's style of argument. Bentham did little more than rephrase Hume's arguments.[17] Mill claimed that a man could be rightfully compelled "to bear his fair share in the common defense, or in any other joint work necessary to the interest of the society of which he enjoys the protection";[18] but there is little by way of an explicit defense of this claim to be found in Mill. Even Sidgwick, the most thorough of the classical utilitarians, has little that is helpful to say on the problem.[19]

One might regard the silence of these utilitarian authors on the problem of political obligation as surprising, given the tradition of English moral philosophy within which they developed. On the other hand, this would be to ignore several obvious considerations. First, Hume was widely regarded as having disposed of consent and contract theories, making concern about such theories unnecessary. But second, there was, I think, among utilitarians a feeling that the simplicity of their theory made it unnecessary to say very much about the problem of political obligation. Bentham, for instance, wrote that each subject "should obey, in short, so long as the probable mischiefs of obedience are less than the probable mischiefs of resistance: . . . it is their duty to obey just so long as it is their interest, and no longer."[20] This was the end of the matter, all that needed to be said. The principle of utility was used to test each individual act of obedience according to its expected consequences, and since expected consequences of obedience varied from case to case, there was no need for any more general account of political obligation.

Now, the approach suggested by Bentham's remarks is, in the jargon of recent moral philosophy, act-utilitarian. (Let us understand by act-utilitarianism the theory that an act is right if and only if it produces at least as much total happiness as any alternative open to the agent.) This approach is (at least often) taken by Mill and Sidgwick as well.[j] And a standard complaint about act-utilitarianism has been that it cannot offer a full or satisfactory account of rights and obligations. If, then, these utilitarians had little to say on the problem of political obligation, this might well be the result of their supporting a moral theory incapable of providing a full account of political obligation (of the sort we seek).

Bentham's approach to problems of political obedience fails in obvious ways to yield an account of political obligation. Act-utilitarian calculations, as Bentham suggests, may lead us to conclude that we ought to obey, but they may lead us as well to conclude that we ought to disobey on some other occasion (or perhaps support the political institutions of some other countries). Insofar as the conditions influencing the results of these calculations are by no means constant, we can derive from the simple act-utilitarian approach no moral requirement to support and comply with the political institutions of one's country of residence. There will be no particularized political bonds on this model; at best, it seems, obligations will be to comply when doing so is optimific. The act-utilitarian might, of course, defend supporting and complying with our political institutions as a useful rule of thumb, based on past experience of the consequences of obedience and disobedience. Disobedience, he might argue, routinely has worse consequences than obedience; so where time is short and calculations are complicated, we ought to simply follow our rule of thumb and obey. But the act-utilitarian has not, of course, provided an account of political obligation by making this move. Where the general happiness can obviously be served by disregarding the rule of

[j] I do not, of course, want to claim that Mill and Sidgwick (or even Bentham, for that matter) were consistent act-utilitarians; both obviously complicated the simple act-utilitarian theory considerably, in ways which were not, I think, particularly systematic. But Bentham, Mill, and Sidgwick all suggest act-utilitarian accounts in their primary formulations of the principle of utility. (While Bentham and Mill both talk of "tendencies" in their versions of the principle, this should not be taken to signal rule-utilitarian intentions in either case.)

thumb, we must do so, for the rule has no prescriptive force independent of the principle of utility.[21]

The problems here are, of course, familiar ones to any student of utilitarianism. There is the initial difficulty that, as a "one principle" theory of moral *rightness*, act-utilitarianism appears to be unable to provide any account of *obligation* at all. Attempts to include secondary principles of obligation under the principle of utility seem to either reduce them to mere rules of thumb or incorporate elements of a *rule*-utilitarian theory. Mill's discussion of secondary principles in Chapter 2 of *Utilitarianism* illustrates the difficulty. Equally familiar problems for act-utilitarianism have been thought to arise from its apparent inability to account for the *stringency* of obligations (as Ross and other intuitionists insisted). Obligations do not seem to give way in the face of very slight possible utility gains, yet act-utilitarianism seems committed to such a consequence. The fact that breaking my promise would produce slightly more utility than keeping it is insufficient to warrant breaking the promise; and similar examples can be imagined for other types of obligations.

The literature on these problems is extensive, and I cannot here attend to each point with the care it deserves. What I will do instead is to comment briefly on a recent act-utilitarian discussion of political obligation, one intended to answer the common objections to act-utilitarianism suggested above. Rolf Sartorius, in the most convincing recent defense of the act-utilitarian theory, has argued that act-utilitarianism can in fact avoid the standard charge that "secondary principles of obligation" must on that theory reduce to mere rules of thumb.[22] Sartorius's basic argument can be briefly (and, I hope, not unfairly) recounted as follows: a typical problem that a society of act-utilitarians would face would be a case in which they knew, as a reliable rule of thumb, that a certain kind of conduct normally led to a maximization of social utility (in some specified set of circumstances), while knowing as well that it would be undesirable to have each person acting on his determination of exceptions to the rule (because of the difficulty of such calculations, attempts to determine exceptions to the rule of thumb would lead more often than not to mistakes). It is, Sartorius argues, perfectly consistent for an act-utilitarian in such a case to participate in elevating the rule of thumb to the status of a norm, backed by sanctions. The sanctions applicable for disobedience to the rule will then restructure the calculations an act-utilitarian will make regarding the conduct in question, leading him to obey the rule (on act-utilitarian grounds) where he might not otherwise have done so. Both the creation of the norm and obedience to it will be justifiable to an act-utilitarian, with the end result that the frequent mistakes in calculation will be eliminated for an overall utility gain. Further, once such norms are accepted as conventions within the society, others will form legitimate expectations based on the norms, providing an act-utilitarian with further reasons for conforming his behavior to the norms. As a result, the norms come to have for him a much firmer status than mere rules of thumb. Now it is Sartorius's contention that (most) conventional rules of obligation satisfy the conditions mentioned above, and consequently that these rules can be supported more fully than mere rules of thumb by a consistent act-utilitarian. Specifically, the act-utilitarian can support and conform his behavior to rules which prohibit a direct appeal to act-utilitarian calculations in determining allowable exceptions (e.g., the rule to keep promises).

How does this argument affect the act-utilitarian's account of political obligation? The argument must be, as it appears to be in Sartorius's discussion,[23] that the rule which requires support and compliance with the political institutions of one's country (and bars appeals to the utility of noncompliance) could be consistently supported by an act-utilitarian, so long as a system of expectations is based on the rule or social sanctions are attached to it, thus altering the utility of supporting it. Does this, if true, mean that the act-utilitarian can in fact provide an account of political obligation of the sort we want? I do not think that it does. There are, first, serious difficulties with Sartorius's general claim to have presented an account of rights and obligations which squares with our ordinary notions.[24] As far as specifically political obligations are concerned, we must remember that only in one limited sense can Sartorius's useful rules be "adopted" by act-utilitarians; while the act of adopting the rule may be one an act-utilitarian should perform, this "adoption" does not confer on the rules (or norms) any new prescriptive force. It merely alters the consequences of disobedience in such a way as to place heavier weight on the side of obedience, because expectations tend to conform to these rules and frustrations (plus the employment of social sanctions) tend to accompany disobedience. The exist-ence of the rule, then, will give act-utilitarians a reason for obeying it, in the limited sense that it becomes reasonable to assume that expectations of others may be frustrated by disobedience. But this reasonable assumption is not necessarily borne out in particular cases; where it is not, and where social sanctions are ineffective, the "obliga-tion" to obey the rule can be seen not to constitute a firm bond of the sort we want. Where the rule in question is that of supporting and complying with political institu-tions, the act-utilitarian view will not provide a moral bond which could be associated with, for instance, the idea of citizenship. This will be true even where the con-ditions for political community are ideal. Again, we are led to conclude that while the act-utilitarian can offer a theory of moral rightness of considerable plausibility, in-termediate principles of obligation of the standard sort must escape him.

If this is correct, an account of political obligation (in our strict sense of the term) will not be forthcoming from the act-utilitarian camp, however the theory is elaborated. Again, I must stress that this should not necessarily be taken as a criticism of act-utilitarianism. Indeed, I have considered only the act-utilitarian theory to this point because I regard it as the only form of utilitarianism that can be given a reasonable defense. The work of Lyons, Smart, and others seems to me thoroughly persuasive in its rejection of the various forms of rule-utilitarianism (and utilitarian generalization).[25] As these authors (and others) have suggested, one committed to maximizing social utility could not consistently act on the kinds of rules sanctioned by rule-utilitarianism. While the rule-utilitarian's principles of obligation will have the kind of force we want in providing an account of political obligation, these principles will not be capable of a utilitarian defense. And these principles will be, at any rate, just the kinds of principles we will examine carefully in the remainder of this essay (at least, if rule-utilitarians are to be believed when they claim that their theory yields principles which match those characterizing our considered moral beliefs). I will not, then, make a special effort here to examine the possibility of constructing a rule-utilitarian account of political obligation.[26] The conclusion to which we are pushed, on the basis of the considerations presented in this section, is, I believe, that the kind of account of political obligation we are seeking is not available to the utilitarian.

I have not yet commented on Hume's utilitarian theory of allegiance. Because it is easily the best known presentation of its kind, I hope that these few remarks will not seem out of place here. Unfortunately, Hume's theory of allegiance is just one portion of his more general account of the "artificial virtues" (those virtues which produce in us pleasure or approbation not "naturally" or directly, but only by means of some "artifice or contrivance"). And Hume is not at all clear about his "utilitarian" defense of these virtues. Bentham, as we have seen, seems to have read Hume's discussion of the artificial virtues as essentially act-utilitarian in character. On this reading, one's "duty of allegiance" would require obedience only in those cases where obeying would produce more total happiness than disobeying. Such an interpretation of

Hume is, at least on the surface, unpromising. For a point which Hume appears to stress repeatedly is that while any particular "naturally virtuous" act (or character trait) is useful (or agreeable), particular "artificially virtuous" acts need *not* be useful; the usefulness of artificially virtuous acts lies in the general performance of such acts. This seems to point to an "indirect" or rule-utilitarian approach to the artificial virtues, one on which we might be bound to perform particular acts which were not useful (or utility maximizing).

Accordingly, many more recent interpretations of Hume have denied the simple act-utilitarian reading which I have attributed to Bentham. Jonathan Harrison, for instance, has found in Hume's work the spirit of a "utilitarian generalizer"; the reason we should be artificially virtuous is that the general practice of such virtuous behavior would have very good consequences (though particular virtuous acts might not).[27] Similarly, John Rawls gives Hume credit for insights which might back a limited form of "conventional rule utilitarianism."[28]

None of the recent "indirect" utilitarian interpretations is, I think, correct. Bentham saw more clearly into Hume's strategy than a casual consideration of his interpretation might indicate. Hume's point about artificial virtues is *not* (as it first appears) that particular virtuous acts may not in fact be useful; it is rather only that they may not be useful in any immediately obvious fashion. The connection between justice (or allegiance) and utility is an always direct but often subtle connection, as many passages in the *Treatise* (and elsewhere) suggest.[29] Admittedly, only an exaggerated sense of the disutility involved in individual violations of these fundamental rules of justice and allegiance could produce an overall position like Hume's. Nonetheless, it is, I think, quite clearly the view Hume advanced. Hume's position on the problem of political obligation, consequently, differs from Bentham's only in Hume's very conservative assumption that the disutilities of disobedience in particular cases are great enough to justify disobedience in only the most extreme political nightmares. For instance, Hume observes:

> We ought always to weigh the advantages which we reap from authority against the disadvantages; and by this means we shall become more scrupulous of putting in practice the doctrine of resistance. The common rule requires submission; and it is only in cases of grievous tyranny and oppression that the exception can take place.[30]

This is, in my view, no more than the "rule of thumb" modification of the simple Benthamic view, an option we discussed earlier. If I am right in this, Hume's utilitarian theory of allegiance will not, as we have seen in Bentham's case, be an account of political obligation of the kind we seek. Whether this constitutes a defect in Hume's position, however, remains to be determined.

II.iv. The Standards of Success

My discussion in II.i and II.ii was designed to clarify the object and the limits of my inquiry, and to justify the strategy I have chosen. And this, as I suggested earlier, is no insignificant task; the enormous variety of conceptions of "the problem of political obligation" displayed in the literature suggests that such preliminaries are imperative. I am, of course, aware that my approach is a somewhat unorthodox one, especially as far as the "particularity requirement" is concerned. This requirement rules out a large number of widely supported answers to questions about political obligation. In addition, I have not accepted answers which treat these questions as questions about "political language."

I am left only with a number of answers which fall squarely within the mainstream of liberal political theory. I will examine what I take to be the four most plausible answers in that tradition: consent theory, the principle of fair play, John Rawls's "Natural Duty of Justice," and principles of gratitude or repayment. Chapters III and IV will be devoted to the consent tradition and its problems; surely this has been, historically at least, the most important approach to the problem of political obligation. Because consent theory relies only on deliberate undertakings as the grounds of political obligation, there is a sense (which I will discuss momentarily) in which consent theory provides an ideal sort of model for a theory of political obligation.

In Chapters V, VI, and VII, I will discuss the remaining three options in turn. In the process, I will show how these accounts can be seen to grow out of or develop certain of the basic intuitions in which consent theory is grounded. I will arrive, then, at a conclusion as to whether political theory can, within the limits I have specified, offer a successful account of our political bonds. There will, I think, be three criteria for the "success" of an account of political obligation. All have been suggested at some point in this chapter. Let us say, first, that an account is "accurate" if it identifies as politically bound those individuals falling within the proper scope of the principle(s) it utilizes; an "accurate" account uses plausible principles of duty or obligation in their most defensible form and applies them correctly. And we will call an account "complete" if it identifies as bound all and only those who are so bound (regardless of its "accuracy"). An "accurate" account can fail to be "complete" by ignoring applicable principles, while a "complete" account can fail to be "accurate" by utilizing implausible or inadequately developed principles. But a wider criterion of success requires that an account be not only accurate and complete, but that it be reasonably general in its application, that is, that it entail that most (or at least many) citizens in most (or many) states are politically bound. While I am not personally dedicated to finding such a general account (I would settle for one that is accurate and com-

plete, no matter how general its application), it is clear
that most of those who have advanced accounts of political obligation have regarded generality (or even "universality," as suggested above in II.i) as the primary criterion
of success. We can, then, adopt this wider criterion of
success as a general standard against which to measure
suggested accounts. Insofar as an account fails this test of
generality, it fails to fill the role in political theory which
an account of political obligation has been thought to fill
by most political theorists. My strategy in the chapters to
follow will be simple; I will attempt to render accurate the
accounts being considered, and then ask whether these
accounts are complete or general in their application. By
considering the four accounts of political obligation
which appear to remain as the only plausible candidates,
and by revising these accounts (where necessary) to make
them accurate, we should be able to arrive at a complete
and accurate account of political obligation. Whether
such an account will be successful in the wider sense remains to be seen. But if it is not, any further attempts at a
"successful" account appear doomed to failure; for if
none of the four accounts I will consider succeeds, or if
they do not somehow succeed jointly, I can see nowhere
else to turn.

CHAPTER III

The Consent Tradition

III.i. Consent Theory

Consent theory has provided us with a more intuitively appealing account of political obligation than any other tradition in modern political theory. At least since Locke's impassioned defense of the natural freedom of men born into nonnatural states, the doctrine of personal consent has dominated both ordinary and philosophical thinking on the subject of our political bonds. The heart of this doctrine is the claim that no man is obligated to support or comply with any political power unless he has personally consented to its authority over him; the classic formulation of the doctrine appears in Locke's *Second Treatise of Government*. There is no denying the attractiveness of the doctrine of personal consent (and of the parallel thesis that no government is legitimate which governs without the consent of the governed). It has greatly influenced the political institutions of many modern states and has been a prime factor in the direction political theory has taken since 1600. But neither can we ignore the manifold difficulties inherent in a consent theory approach to the problem of political obligation, which have been well known since Hume's attack on the social contract.[1] The present chapter and Chapter IV will be directed toward a clarification and evaluation of this consent theory account of political obligation.

When I speak of "consent theory," I will mean any theory of political obligation which maintains that the political obligations of citizens are grounded in their personal performance of a voluntary act which is the deliberate undertaking of an obligation. Thus, theories which ground political obligations in promises, contracts, or express or tacit consent will all count as varieties of "consent theory." In the language of Chapter I, consent theorists are those who regard political obligations as "obligations of commitment." There are, as I suggested, views concerning political authority which are usually (but not always) conjoined with a consent theory account of political obligation. Most consent theorists also maintained that all de jure political authority arises from the same deliberate undertaking which generates the political obligations of each citizen. The community grants the government its authority; a government which has not been granted authority by the consent or contracts of its citizens cannot be legitimate. I will have more to say about this view of governmental legitimacy in VIII.ii. I mention it here only because the rise of consent theory in the history of political thought coincided with the rise of this view of political authority and the legitimacy of government. For on the standard consent model, as I noted above, the notions of political obligation and political authority were thought to be "correlative," in the sense that the undertaking of each political obligation entailed the granting of political authority (and vice versa).

Prior to the rise of consent theory, of course, the standard views of political authority and political obligation were quite different.[2] The doctrine of St. Paul was nearly universally accepted, by political theorist and layman alike:

> Let every person be subject to the governing authorities. For there is no authority except from God, and those that exist have been instituted by God. Therefore he who resists the authorities resists what God has appointed, and those who resist will incur judgment.[3]

The political authority of kings was believed to be granted by God, and the duties of citizens toward their king were imposed by God. Neither the conduct of kings nor the behavior of individual citizens played any part in the generation of political bonds or authority.

It was in reaction to this view, and the passive and unconditional obedience by the citizen which it commanded, that consent theory and the corresponding doctrine of political authority arose, amid the unrest and rebellion of the seventeenth and eighteenth centuries.[4] The analysis of social and political institutions in terms of "consent" or "contract" is thus primarily a modern approach (although there are some ancient writings which at least point in this direction, e.g., several of Plato's dialogues and the peculiar individualism of Epicurus).[5] There were, of course, a number of rudimentary "social contract theories" within the vein of medieval thought. The "Vindiciae contra tyrannos" (1579), for example, discusses "the contract" between king and citizens; but political authority and political obligations still retain a religious base.[6] And in general, when "consent" and "contract" were invoked in medieval political theory, their role was somewhat mysterious. As J. W. Gough notes, when it was said that a king governed "with the consent of the barons, or of parliament," it was not meant that the king's authority "was granted to him by them."[7] The notion of "consent" rests uneasily in most medieval political treatises, playing no important role.

It was not until the works of George Buchanan[8] and "the judicious" Richard Hooker,[9] the last of the important medieval political thinkers, that political authority and political obligations were made to rest on the consent of the community. This lead was followed by Johannas Althusius,[10] Hugo Grotius,[11] and John Milton[12] in the early seventeenth century. These were the authors of the first important consent theories, on the foundation of which the classic works of Hobbes, Locke, and Rousseau were constructed.[13]

I want now to look at some of the salient features of consent theory which make it an attractive account of political obligation. After that, I will consider in Chapter IV some of the difficulties which a consent theorist faces. I want to stress here that the discussion of consent theory to follow will not deal with any one writer's actual position. Rather, I will try to understand a shared position, by emphasizing several major points important to a consent theory account of political obligation, points which are agreed upon by nearly all of the classic consent theorists.

It will be useful to begin by distinguishing two strains within the consent tradition, two ways in which consent has been thought to be important to the generation of political obligations. The first approach is embodied in my definition of "consent theory"; political obligations are grounded in the *personal* consent of each citizen who is bound. The second approach we may call a theory of "historical consent." On this approach it is maintained that the political obligations of all citizens (of all times) within a state are generated by the consent of the members of the *first* generation of the political community. Political theorists who have written of an "original contract" often have such an approach to political obligation in mind. This is explicitly the position of Hooker, and hints of a theory of "historical consent" abound within the treatises of Hobbes and Rousseau.

But of course, such a theory is very implausible, as Hume made clear (later, in a more thorough fashion, Kant did the same).[14] The obvious difficulty is that only in very special circumstances can the consent of one individual bind some other individual (even if this latter individual is a descendant of the former).[15] Such circumstances arise when the person who gives consent has been *authorized* by another to act for him on the matter. And clearly the descendants of the "original contractors" could not have authorized the making of an original contract! So it seems clear that this particular line of argument within the consent tradition will take us nowhere, and that only the "personal consent" line needs to be considered seriously (with provisions, of course, for allowing "personal consent" to be given by an agent).[16]

A more plausible variant of the argument from historical consent maintains that the history of a state must include the performance of a "contract of government" (a contract between ruler and ruled which establishes the rights and duties of each party) in order for that state's government to be legitimate. I call this variant "more plausible" only because it continues by concluding that an original contract is only a *necessary* condition for the political obligations of future citizens. This conclusion follows if one holds that no political obligations can be owed to an illegitimate government, and that it is at least possible that even a government which did originate in a contract is not owed such obligations.

But the plausibility which I ascribed to this variant is slight. The notion of "legitimacy" utilized in the argument seems quite unrealistic. In the first place, it condemns nearly all governments to illegitimacy (since such original contracts are at best rare). And even if this result is not obviously objectionable, the means of reaching it are. For it would seem very foolish to hold that even a *perfect* government was illegitimate, simply because it did not originate in a contract of government (or that a government could not *be* perfect simply because it did not so originate). I will have more to say about this problem of obligation and legitimacy in III.iv and VIII.ii.

III.ii. The Major Assumptions

According to the consent theory account, our political obligations arise from our personally consenting (or having authorized another who consents for us) to the government's authority. A more precise explanation of what it means to consent to something follows in Chapter IV. Here I wish to discuss what I take to be the four central theses which a consent theory characteristically advances in developing its position, and to clarify their relation to the consent theory account of political obligation.

1. *Man is naturally free*. This important claim is too often rejected unthinkingly as a part of the myth of a "state of nature"; but clearly its significance is greater than that of the myth within the context of which it was frequently presented. What exactly do we mean when we claim that man is "naturally free," as Rousseau did, in the famous opening to his *Social Contract* (which became a battle cry for French revolutionary writers): "Man is born free; and everywhere he is in chains. . . . How did this change come about? I do not know. What can make it legitimate? That question I think I can answer."[17] When Rousseau claims that man is "born free," he does not mean that when a man is born there are no obstacles to the fulfillment of his desires; nor does he mean, I think, even that there are no *moral* constraints on his actions.[k] Rousseau's concern is with the legitimacy of governmental coercion of the individual within certain areas, and his claim is that all men have a *right* to freedom of action within these areas. The central question of Book I of the *Social Contract*, as Rousseau states it, is under what conditions the right of freedom, which governments do in fact transgress, can be *legitimately* transferred or overridden? He answers that only when this right is given up voluntarily through consent to the government's control, can governments legitimately coerce individuals within these (as yet unspecified) areas.

The familiar claim that man is "born free" is normally a claim about a "natural right" man is supposed to possess. In calling a right "natural," we mean, first, that it is possessed by all men (or "all rational agents," or "all agents capable of choice") solely by virtue of their humanity (or "rational agency," or "power of choice"). And second, a

---

[k] Rousseau does, of course, sometimes deny the existence of natural moral bonds. But this must be viewed as a confusion, in light of his need for natural law to explain the force of the social contract.

"natural right" is not the product of some voluntary act, as other sorts of rights are. The natural right in question here is the "natural right of freedom," the right to act as one chooses within the limits of "natural law," without interference (in the form of coercion or restraint) from others.[18]

It is, then, a bit misleading to say that man is "born free" when one means that man has a "natural right of freedom." For being "naturally free" in this sense still leaves man bound by the rules of "natural law," what we have called the "natural duties" (duties which all men have simply by virtue of their humanity). But this seems to be exactly what is meant by references to "natural freedom" or "being born free" both in the writings of political philosophers and in many political documents whose drafting was influenced by these writings.[19] Most of the major writers in the consent tradition share Rousseau's views about man's "natural freedom." Thus, we find Hobbes defending "the Right of Nature," as "the liberty each man has to use his own power . . . for the preservation of his own nature";[20] and Locke stating, "we must consider what state all men are naturally in, and that is, a state of perfect freedom to order their actions . . . within the bounds of the Law of Nature";[21] and Kant claiming that: "Freedom . . . , insofar as it is compatible with the freedom of everyone else in accordance with a universal law, is the one sole and original right that belongs to every human being by virtue of his humanity."[22] The "natural freedom" of man, then, is something less than "perfect" freedom; it is a freedom limited by the "natural duties" which each man has (the rules of "natural law," for which the categorical imperative stands in in Kant's theory).

Consent theory recognized a distinction between two sorts of moral bonds, the natural and the "special," and denied that political obligation could be *natural*. The "special" obligations are those which arise from an individual's voluntarily entering some "special relationship or transaction."[23] Only by such voluntary actions does a man leave his "natural state of freedom." If, then, an individual's political bonds are "special obligations," his political obligations cannot be inherited, or thrust upon him at birth, but can only be the product of his own voluntary actions. And my remarks in Chapter II concerning the "particularity requirement" supported the conclusion that political obligations *are* special obligations; only a special obligation can bind the citizen to the state in which he resides above all others. This is a fact which the consent tradition recognized.

The claim that man is naturally free, then, connects in obvious ways to consent theory's contention that our political bonds must be freely assumed. And in this respect, the "state of nature" is a useful device. It describes men prior to their having voluntarily acted in ways which bind them and provides a new way of talking about the intuitive distinction between duties and obligations.

2. *Man gives up his natural freedom (and is bound by obligations) only by voluntarily giving a "clear sign" that he desires to do so.* This claim has, in part, been anticipated in thesis 1 above. It reaffirms the "will-dependence" of obligations which the consent tradition recognized. Obligations (for the consent theorist) not only require the performance of voluntary acts,[24] but require that these acts be *deliberate* undertakings; an individual cannot become obligated unless he intentionally performs an obligation-generating act with a clear understanding of its significance. Thus, the ground of all obligations must be the giving of a "clear sign" of the appropriate sort to indicate the acceptance of the obligation and the transfer of right. In Hobbes's words, "the way by which a man either simply renounces or transfers his right is a declaration or signification by some voluntary and sufficient sign or signs that he does so renounce or transfer."[25]

Because, for the consent theorists, our political bonds are *obligations*, this means that each man is free to choose for himself (upon reaching the "age of consent") to accept political obligations or not. And only a deliberate act of consent (or contract, or promise) will suffice to indicate that such obligations have been chosen. The varieties of consent, express and tacit, will be discussed in Chapter IV. But all types of consent must be deliberate undertakings, sufficient to indicate clearly that the actor has freely given up his natural freedom with respect to the specified actions and parties.

It should also be noted here that to the consent theory account of political obligation is often added the claim that giving one's consent to a government's authority involves no "net loss" of freedom. In fact, this is seen as the major merit of the method of consent by several consent theorists. For while the individual gives up his natural freedom (to some extent) in authorizing the government to direct his actions, he allegedly both gains in the "new freedom" available under the rule of law, and also, since his authorization "makes the government's acts his own," does not really lose any freedom of action to begin with.[26] This is the spirit in which Rousseau names as "the fundamental problem of which the Social Contract provides the solution" that of finding "a form of association . . . in which each, while uniting himself with all, may still obey himself alone, and remain as free as before."[27] Kant follows Rousseau's suggestion on this point,[28] and the strategy is also found, although less clearly, in Locke and Hobbes. This peculiar and implausible argument, fortunately, is not a necessary part of a consent theory and need not concern us here; the real value of the consent theory approach to the problem of political obligation lies elsewhere, as I will suggest momentarily.

3. *The method of consent protects the citizen from injury by the state.* This claim is advanced, either explicitly or implicitly, by nearly every consent theorist, as it is thought to constitute one of the (if not the) chief virtues of the method of consent. But there are two versions in which this claim is advanced. The first version holds that by making consent necessary for political obligation, we guarantee that only a government which has been "cho-

sen" by the individual has any legitimate power over him. Thus, he is protected from being automatically bound at birth, and from becoming bound unknowingly, to a tyrannical or unjust government. This "protection" is certainly one of the most attractive features of the consent theory account of political obligation.

The second version of this claim turns it into a logical point about the consequences of giving consent to a government; as such, it does not really concern "protection" at all. This version of the claim runs as follows: the method of consent guarantees that a government which *has* been consented to can never (logically) injure (in the classical sense of "wrong") the citizen, provided it is acting "intra vires" (within the terms of the citizen's consent). When the individual freely consents to government control, he indicates that he has taken up his bonds willingly and cannot complain of being held to them. Thus, his consent assures us that the coercive measures of government are legitimate, if they do not overstep the assigned limits. This notion is adequately expressed by a maxim of private law—"volenti non fit injuria"—the willing man is not wronged. Hobbes refers to this maxim in *De Cive*[29] and later restates it in *Leviathan*: "whatsoever is done to a man, conformable to his own will signified to the doer, is no injury to him."[30]

Now, there are at least two difficulties with this doctrine as it appears in the classical expositions of consent theory. First, it is by no means obvious that even giving one's express consent to another's act always justifies his performance (although I do not propose to argue against the claim here); certain sorts of acts might be thought to constitute "injuries" even when consented to. This leads directly to the second difficulty, for consent theorists have in fact, along with the argument outlined above, also wanted to recognize *limits* on the sanctity of personal consent (and thus on their respect for the individual's personal decisions). These limits appear in the doctrine that certain natural rights are "inalienable." Thus, Hobbes

also observes that "a man cannot lay down the right of re-
sisting them that assault him by force to take away his
life."[31] Locke asserts that "a man . . . cannot subject himself to the arbitrary power of another."[32] For Locke, even
the clearest case of express consent to become a slave
cannot make wrong a man's resistance to his master or
right the master's enforcing the enslavement.[l] Similarly,
Kant holds that no contract could put a man "into the
class of domestic animals which we use at will for any
kind of service";[33] that is because "every man has inalienable rights which he cannot give up even if he would."[34]

Quite aside from the difficulty that Sidgwick notes of
"deducing these inalienable rights from any clear and
generally accepted principles,"[35] this line of argument is
a difficult one for the consent theorist to maintain. For
where on the one hand the consent theorist shows great
respect for the individual's decisions ("volenti non fit
injuria"—consent is sufficient to transfer any right), the
doctrine of inalienable rights threatens this respect (consent is not sufficient to transfer some rights). Why, for instance, should a man not be free to enslave himself if he so
desires, or to allow another to rightfully take his life?
Hobbes argues that "of the voluntary acts of every man,
the object is some good to himself. And therefore there be
some rights which no man can be understood by any
words or other signs to have abandoned or transferred";
consenting sometimes amounts to a sort of contradiction,
for a man who consents to be killed seems to "despoil
himself of the end for which those signs were intended."[36] Although the basic premise on which the ar-

[l] I mention these remarks in this context because they are often taken
to indicate that Locke advanced a theory of inalienable rights. In fact,
Locke denies the possibility of absolute power because it implies the
transfer of a right (to take one's life as one pleases) which no man pos-
sesses. There is simply no such right held by men, rather than a right
held by them which is inalienable. On the other hand, there is evidence
that Locke believes that some of those rights we do possess naturally can
only be transferred to another in part; and this does suggest a theory of
inalienable rights.

gument is based (i.e., that the object of every voluntary act is some good for the actor) is quite implausible, we could accept it and still reply as follows within the spirit of consent theory: who are we to decide that even a man's giving up his right of self-defense might not constitute "some good to himself"? For, in the first place, my giving up a right does not guarantee that it will be used against me. (Might it not be "some good to me" to trade my "right of self-defense" to my best friend for $100, knowing that he would never try to harm me even though he had the right?) But secondly, the chief reason that consent theory does not allow men to be automatically bound at birth to *any* state (even an ideal state, whose only concern is for the interests of its members), is that no one may decide what is in the interest of another (see thesis 4 below).

There are, of course, other arguments for inalienable rights.[37] But this is a complex issue, and I wish to suggest here only that the doctrine of inalienable rights fits uncomfortably into a consent theory, for it smacks of a paternalism that consent theorists, above all others, have opposed. And while I know of no good arguments, within the consent tradition or without, for the existence of inalienable rights, this is not the place to argue that there are no such arguments.

4. *The state is an instrument for serving the interests of its citizens.* The state's authority is "given" to it by its citizens, who decide both whether the state will serve their interests, and how to balance freedom within the state against benefits provided. Neither the state nor any person is free to decide what is in the interest of another. Only by giving his consent, and so indicating that he finds the government to be such that it will serve his interests to become a citizen, does a man become one who can be rightfully governed. (As suggested above, the fear of misplaced paternalism is a central motivation for the development of a consent theory. One need only read Locke's *Two Treatises* to be convinced of this fact.) Thus,

even if a man is born into a *perfect* state, he remains free not to assume those bonds of obedience and support which would make him a member of the political community.

Consent theory, then, is not solely concerned with protecting the individual from injury by the state, although this protective function naturally takes a central position. Rather, the method of consent protects the individual from becoming bound to any government which he finds unpalatable, be it a good one or a bad one, one which injures him or one which *protects* him from injury. What is protected, then, is not primarily the individual himself, or his interests, but rather his freedom to *choose* whether to become bound to a particular government (commonly, the government of the country in which he is born and raised). The consent theorist demonstrates a preference for *individual commitment* over unavoidable benefits or protection of interests. It is this preference that marks consent theory as a *liberal* theory; for the priority of liberty over (forced) happiness is the hallmark of political liberalism.

The appeal of the position described through these four theses is obvious. Consent theory respects our belief that the course a man's life takes should be determined, as much as possible, by his own decisions and actions.[38] Since being born into a political community is neither an act we perform, nor the result of a decision we have made, we feel that this should not limit our freedom by automatically binding us to the government of that community. And these convictions serve as the basis of a theory of political obligation which holds that only the voluntary giving of a clear sign that one finds the state acceptable (and is willing to assume political bonds to it) can ever obligate one to support or comply with the commands of that state's government.

There is a sense in which consent theory might be

thought not just appealing, but to be the ideal account of political obligation. Consent theory has fastened on the promise as the model for the grounds of political obligation. The feature that promises, contracts, and the giving of consent share is that they are all deliberate undertakings. These are all acts that can only be performed intentionally and knowingly. By showing, for instance, that a promise was made without any awareness that an obligation was being undertaken in the process, we defeat the claim that a promise was ever made. Contracts and acts of giving one's consent share with promising this special vulnerability to "infelicities" of the sort that Austin labels "Misfires."[39] One must know what one is doing in order to perform these sorts of acts.

By using deliberate undertakings as the grounds of political obligation, consent theory includes two very desirable features. First (as mentioned previously), consent theory maximizes protection of the individual's freedom to choose where his political allegiance will lie. Political obligations cannot be inherited or unwittingly acquired. And a deliberate undertaking, of which promising is the paradigm, is the only ground of obligation which allows this feature to be present in a theory of political obligation. Second, the model of the promise lends clarity and credibility to a theory of political obligation; for promising is surely as close to being an indisputable ground of moral requirement as anything is. Basing a theory of political obligation on consent, then, lends it plausibility unequaled by rival theories.

These facts suggest that there is ample justification for the central place in modern political theory which consent theory has occupied. And they help to explain the wide support, both in philosophical and nonphilosophical settings, that consent theory has received. But consent theory is not, as any student of political philosophy knows, an approach devoid of difficulties. It is with these difficulties that Chapter IV will deal.

III.iii. Majority Consent

In III.i we discussed some of the difficulties involved in a doctrine of "historical consent." In III.ii we considered the theory based on "personal consent." But there remains another line of argument prominent in the consent tradition which concerns "majority consent." The problem of majority consent can best be understood in terms of a problem concerning legitimacy with which consent theorists took themselves to be faced. As I mentioned earlier (III.i), the consent theorist's position on governmental legitimacy has normally been that legitimacy depends on the consent of the governed. A government has authority only over those citizens who have granted that authority through their consent, and only a government which has authority over all of its citizens is legitimate. Thus, a legitimate government must have the unanimous consent of its citizens. This is the conclusion to which the consent theorist is inevitably led, for he allows neither that political authority can derive from any source other than consent, nor that legitimacy can be, e.g., relative to particular citizens (i.e., a government must be, for the consent theorist, either legitimate or not).

But this, it is easy to see, makes a government's legitimacy or illegitimacy turn implausibly on the possibility of one citizen refusing to give his consent. And further, if one citizen did refuse to give his consent to the government's authority, thereby rendering his government illegitimate, then even the consenting individuals would not be obligated, for no one can be bound to an illegitimate government (or so the classic consent theorists maintained). These are conclusions which the consent theorist was concerned to avoid. One way of avoiding them is by adopting a doctrine of "majority consent," and many consent theorists seem to have taken that course.

The doctrine of majority consent offers a way of making governmental legitimacy depend on consent, while avoiding the consequences of requiring unanimous consent. Alan Gewirth notes:

> It is significant that not only Hobbes but also Locke and Rousseau drop unanimous consent from further consideration as soon as they have used it to justify the institution of the political community and government as such, and they assign to the majority the effective choice of and consent to the specific government.[40]

Thus, Rousseau asserts that while the original contract "needs unanimous consent . . . , apart from this primitive contract, the vote of the majority always binds the rest."[41] And, as Gewirth pointed out, in this claim Rousseau is in agreement with Hobbes[42] and Locke.[43] The position being defended, then, seems to be that government legitimacy rests on the consent of a majority of the citizens. But because a government is legitimate if and only if all citizens are obligated to it (for these theorists), Rousseau, Hobbes, and Locke must, it seems, also defend the view that *all* citizens have political obligations if the *majority* give their consent. The paradoxical feature of this position, of course, is that it entails that some individuals may become bound to a government to which they have not personally consented; the personal consent of those in the majority will suffice to bind them.

This conclusion, however, is in diametrical opposition to all that consent theory stressed originally concerning political obligation—namely, that no man can be bound to any government except by his personal consent. Yet the doctrine of majority consent is also one which has come down to us through the consent tradition to form a part of those liberal political principles recognized by nonphilosophers. The question is: how can consent theorists have presented together two positions so obviously in conflict? One sort of answer amounts to an accusation of political conservatism; these theorists preferred to undermine their own insistence on personal consent as the sole ground of political obligation, rather than face the possibility that no governments would turn out to be legitimate, owing to a lack of unanimous consent.[m] But a more generous reading of the texts cited seems to point to another answer. Majority consent is only supposed to bind the *original* contractors in their choice of a government; it is not meant to be significant for later generations at all. Thus, the original contractors unanimously agree to come together to create a government, and, after this original agreement, are all bound to accept whatever *particular* form of government is chosen by the majority. The dissenting contractors are bound to the government created in spite of their failure to consent to its authority, and the government created is a legitimate government in spite of this lack of unanimity. But after this first contract (i.e., in the generations to follow) the "doctrine of majority consent" has no significance. Personal consent is required for political obligation and unanimous consent for legitimacy.[n]

But this simply returns us to our original problem. How is the consent theorist to avoid the charge that if unanimous consent is required for legitimacy, no governments will be legitimate? The answer, for Hobbes, Locke, and Rousseau,[44] is found in the notion of "tacit consent through residence." For if mere residence can be taken to be a sign of consent, then unanimous consent is *guaranteed*. This, however, seems to show more than the consent theorist wanted, for it seems to show not just that some governments are after all legitimate, but rather that *all* governments are legitimate. The problem, of course, is

[m] An obvious way out of the consent theorist's dilemma would have been to allow for the possibility of "partial legitimacy," that is, legitimacy with respect to only some citizens. As far as I know, however, this sort of solution was not attempted.

[n] This interpretation seems to be an accurate reading of Hobbes's remarks on majority consent, and also, though less certainly, of Locke's. With Rousseau, however, I am not at all confident that this explanation captures his intentions.

that in order to find some "sign of consent" which all citizens in *some* states could be taken to have given, Hobbes, Locke, and Rousseau were forced to accept one which all citizens in *all* states could be taken to have given. But we need not dwell on this problem any longer here, for it will be, in part, the subject of Chapter IV. I introduce the problem here only in order to show one possible reason (the difficulties with governmental legitimacy) a consent theorist might have for relying on "tacit consent through residence."

CHAPTER IV

The Argument
from Tacit Consent

IV.i. Consent Defined

In Chapter III we tried to locate that which was most convincing in the arguments presented by consent theorists. A number of fruitless developments in consent theory were rejected in favor of the doctrine of personal consent, the view that no man is obligated to support or comply with any political power unless he has personally consented to its authority over him. And we showed why this consent theory account of political obligation has been persuasive and appealing.

In this chapter I will examine critically the consent theory account, after first giving a brief explanation of what we mean when we say that a man "consented" and "tacitly consented" to something. Locke's consent theory will serve as a focal point for my discussion, and I will challenge a recent interpretation of it which calls into question Locke's status as a genuine consent theorist. By drawing distinctions between two senses of "consent" and between two sorts of acts generally taken to be consensual in character, I will expose the major defects both of consent theory and of most contemporary discussions of consent theory. Finally, in IV.iv, I will return to a more thorough examination of the possibilities of realizing a political system in which residence constitutes consent to the government's authority.

Let me begin, then, by considering briefly just what it means to say that a man has "given his consent" to something or someone. In Locke's discussion in his *Second Treatise*, we can distinguish (although Locke himself does not) three sorts of acts which count for him as acts of consent. First, there are promises; second, there are written contracts; and third, there are acts of consent which are essentially authorizations of the actions of others. My own inclination is to say that of the three, only the third sort of act is a genuine act of consent. But there are certainly good reasons for grouping the three together. All are deliberate, voluntary acts whose understood purpose is to change the structure of rights of the parties involved and to generate obligations for the "consentors." In addition, there is a perfectly natural and acceptable sense of the word "consent" which is virtually synonymous with "promise"; thus, when we say that Mr. Smiley has graciously consented to speak at the award dinner, "consented" means here precisely "promised" or "agreed."

My discussion of consent, however, will treat this sense as a secondary one. We will be interested here in a kind of consent that differs from promising in a number of ways. First, consent in the strict sense (as Plamenatz rightly notes)[1] is always given to the actions of other persons. Thus, I may consent to my daughter's marriage, to be governed by the decisions of the majority, or to my friend's handling my financial affairs. Promises, on the other hand, cannot, except in very special circumstances, ever be made concerning the actions of another person. Further, while both promises and consent generate special rights and obligations, the emphases in the two cases are different. The primary purpose of a promise is to undertake an obligation; the special rights which arise for the promisee are in a sense secondary. In giving consent to another's actions, however, our primary purpose is to authorize those actions and in so doing create for or accord to another a special right to act; the obligation generated on the consentor not to interfere with the exercise of this right takes, in this case, the secondary role.

Now, I do not wish to appear to be making too much of this distinction. I call attention to it only because in the discussion to follow a number of problems arise which concern consent in this strict sense, but not promising.

These problems revolve around the "intentionality" of consent and have caused considerable confusion for political theorists. So while my conclusions concerning the suitability of consent as a ground for political obligation will apply as well to promising or contracting (that is, to all the grounds of "obligations of commitment"), I will hereafter be considering primarily consent in the strict sense, in an effort to approach these confusions as painlessly as possible. When I speak of consenting, then, I will mean the according to another by the consentor of a special right to act within areas within which only the consentor is normally free to act; this is accomplished through a suitable expression of the consentor's intention to enter such a transaction and involves the assuming of a special obligation not to interfere with the exercise of the right accorded.[2]

As with promising, of course, I may give my consent by any number of means. Words, gestures, and lack of response are all suitable methods in appropriate contexts. I propose not to dwell here on the contextual and procedural conditions necessary for consenting. Insofar as these conditions can be specified at all, they are similar to those for promising (which have received considerable attention elsewhere).[3] Rather, I wish to emphasize only two general conditions, which will figure in later discussion. First, consent must be given intentionally and (perhaps this is redundant) knowingly. As with promising, one can consent insincerely, but not unintentionally. Second, consent must be given voluntarily. It is not possible to be very precise about this condition, but there are at least obvious cases on either side of a very fuzzy line; "consent" which is given under the direct threat of serious physical violence is, for instance, not really consent according to this condition.

Before turning to tacit consent, I want to mention one recent interpretation of this voluntariness condition which makes a mistake of particular importance to a consent theory account of political obligation. John Rawls, in

A Theory of Justice, maintains that "acquiescence in, or even consent to, clearly unjust institutions does not give rise to obligations,"[4] and that "obligatory ties presuppose just institutions."[5] Rawls defends this initially plausible position as follows: "It is generally agreed that extorted promises are void ab initio. But similarly, unjust social arrangements are themselves a kind of extortion, even violence, and consent to them does not bind."[6] This argument seems to me to be a good illustration of the dangers of metaphor. That unjust institutions perpetrate "violence" on innocents does not necessarily have anything to do with the conditions under which one consents, which is what is at issue here. Extorted promises fail to bind because they are not made voluntarily in the appropriate sense; but the injustice of an institution need not affect the voluntariness of one's consent to it. Supposing only that the unjust institution does not happen to be doing violence to *me*, I can freely consent to its authority.

To see this, we need only consider that a parallel argument would seem to commit Rawls to the position that a promise to an unscrupulous villain does not bind; but this, of course, is absurd. A man's bad moral character cannot, by itself, free us from commitments we make to him. A promise to aid him in his villainy, of course, would not bind us. But here it is the content of the promise, not the character of the promisee, which prevents the generation of an obligation. And these suggestions about villainous men seem to hold as well for "villainous" institutions. We can, however, appreciate the sentiments that might support Rawls's claim, for surely we ought not to support intolerably unjust institutions. But it seems more natural to allow that we can sometimes succeed in obligating ourselves both by promises to villains and by consent to "autocratic and arbitrary forms of government" (to borrow Rawls's phrase). In addition, however, we have a clear duty both to help confound villainy and to fight injustice. Thus, it will be a matter for decision in individual cases whether, e.g., the harm done by supporting an unjust institution and our duty to fight injustice outweigh any obligation we may have to respect its authority (deriving from our consent to it). I maintain, then, that it is at least possible for a person to bind himself to an unjust institution through a deliberate act of consent. (Note that this position does not, however, involve moving to the opposite and objectionable extreme of suggesting that *all* acts of consent are sufficient to generate obligations.)

IV.ii. Tacit Consent

Since the earliest consent theories it has of course been recognized that "express consent" is not a suitably general ground for political obligation. The paucity of express consentors is painfully apparent. Most of us have never been faced with a situation where express consent to a government's authority was even appropriate, let alone actually performed such an act. And while I think that most of us agree that express consent is *a* ground of political obligation (and certainly this is my view), the real battleground for consent theory is generally admitted to be the notion of tacit consent. It is on this leg that consent theory must lean most heavily if it is to succeed.

Thomas Hobbes noted that "signs of contract are either express or by inference,"[7] but he had little clear to say about this distinction. Discussions of tacit consent since that time have generally added only confusions to Hobbes's lack of clarity. Certainly Locke's discussion of tacit consent has puzzled many political philosophers by stretching the notion of consent far beyond the breaking point. But we must not be led by these confusions to believe that there is no such thing as tacit consent. On the contrary, genuine instances of tacit consent, at least in nonpolitical contexts, are relatively frequent.

Consider: Chairman Jones stands at the close of the company's board meeting and announces, "There will be a meeting of the board at which attendance will be mandatory next Tuesday at 8:00, rather than at our usual Thursday time. Any objections?" The board members remain silent. In remaining silent and inactive, they have all tacitly consented to the chairman's proposal to make a schedule change (assuming, of course, that none of the members is asleep, or failed to hear, etc.). As a result, they have given the chairman the right (which he does not normally have) to reschedule the meeting, and they have undertaken the obligation to attend at the new time.

Now this example should allow us to elaborate more constructively on the conditions necessary for tacit consent. First, consent here is called "tacit" not because it has a different sort of significance than express consent, nor because it, e.g., binds less completely (as Locke seems to have thought). Consent is called tacit when it is given by remaining silent and inactive; it is not express, explicit, directly and distinctly expressed by action, but rather is expressed by the failure to do certain things. But tacit consent is nonetheless given or expressed. Silence after a call for objections can be just as much an expression of consent as shouting "aye" after a call for ayes and nayes. Calling consent tacit, then, points only to the special mode of its expression.

But under what conditions can silence be taken as a sign of consent? At least three spring quickly to mind.[8] (1) The situation must be such that it is perfectly clear that consent is appropriate and that the individual is aware of this. This includes the requirement that the potential consentor be awake and aware of what is happening. (2) There must be a definite period of reasonable duration when objections or expressions of dissent are invited or clearly appropriate, and the acceptable means of expressing this dissent must be understood by or made known to the potential consentor. (3) The point at which expressions of dissent are no longer acceptable must be obvious or made clear in some way to the potential consentor. These three conditions seem to jointly guarantee that the potential consentor's silence is *significant*. For they show that the silence does not result simply from (1) a failure to grasp the nature of the situation, (2) a lack of understanding of proper procedures, or (3) a misunderstanding about how long one has to decide whether or not to dissent. If any one of the conditions is not satisfied, then silence may indicate a breakdown in communication of one of these kinds. In that case, silence could not be taken as a sign of consent.

Our example of the board meeting meets these three conditions, although the time period specified in condition 3 is fairly informally and loosely set. In addition, of course, the example seems to meet the more general conditions for the possibility of consent of any sort. But while in most circumstances these conditions are, I think, sufficient, I want to suggest two additional conditions which will be important to the political applications of theory of tacit consent: (4) the means acceptable for indicating dissent must be reasonable and reasonably easily performed; and (5) the consequences of dissent cannot be extremely detrimental to the potential consentor. The violation of either condition 4 or 5 will mean that silence cannot be taken as a sign of consent, even though the other conditions for consent and tacit consent are satisfied.

We can easily imagine situations which would fail to satisfy our new conditions 4 and 5. For instance, if Chairman Jones had, in our previous example, said, "Anyone with an objection to my proposal will kindly so indicate by lopping off his arm at the elbow," both conditions would be violated, as they would be if dissent could only be expressed by resignation and the forfeit of company benefits, etc. Less dramatically, perhaps, condition 4 alone would be violated if board meeting traditions demanded that dissent could only be indicated by turning a perfect back handspring. And if the invariable consequence of objecting at a board meeting was dismissal and imprisonment (Chairman Jones happens also to be the local magistrate), our condition 5 would not be satisfied.

In any of these cases, silence cannot be taken as a sign of

consent. As with all of the previous conditions, it is not possible to draw lines very clearly here; but if, say, the obstacles to consent were only the board members' nervousness about talking to Chairman Jones, or the fear that he might not give them a lift to the train station after the meeting, the situation would pretty clearly not violate conditions 4 and 5.

Of our two new conditions, condition 4, at least, seems unobjectionable. It guarantees that the failure to dissent is not due to an inability to dissent. But condition 5 may be more controversial. For it may seem that where the potential consentor remains silent because of fear or coercion, genuine consent is still given, but is simply a case of genuine consent which is not *binding*. I am not really sure how we could choose between calling a coerced act of consent "genuine but nonbinding" and saying that it is "not really consent at all." Ordinary language, for instance, seems to favor neither option over the other. I have chosen the latter description in order to emphasize the fact that we understand consent to involve a choice freely made (where this "freedom" includes freedom from the immediate threat of dire consequences). But both options agree that coerced consent generates no *obligations*. And because we are concerned here with a consent theory account of political *obligation*, how we choose to handle coerced consent is of little moment to our present task. I will insist, then, on the satisfaction of conditions 1 through 5 inclusive, in order for silence to be taken as a sign of consent. Of course, these conditions need not be satisfied if the consentor somehow *confirms* that the significance of his silence is meant to be the giving of tacit consent. But such confirmations are rarely available and more rarely sought in the specific context with which we will be dealing, namely, that setting in which tacit consent might be given to a government's authority.

I have no doubt, of course, that the expression "tacit consent" is sometimes used in ways that do not conform to the account of tacit consent sketched above; my intention was not primarily to catalog all of the ordinary uses of the expression. Rather, I have tried to present what seems to me to be the only ordinary notion of tacit consent that can be useful to the consent theorist. This account stresses particularly the intentionality of even tacit consent. Only if tacit consent is treated, as I have treated it here, as a *deliberate* undertaking can the real force of consent theory be preserved. For consent theory's account of political obligation is appealing only if consent remains a clear ground of obligation, and if the method of consent protects the individual from becoming politically bound unknowingly or against his will. And it seems clear that these essential features of a consent theory cannot be preserved if we allow that tacit consent can be given unintentionally.

IV.iii. Locke and the Failure of Tacit Consent

Now that we have a reasonably clear notion of tacit consent as a tool, we can approach Locke's account of tacit consent somewhat more confidently.[9] Locke's famous discussion of tacit consent begins as follows: "The difficulty is, what ought to be looked upon as a tacit consent, and how far it binds, i.e., how far any one shall be looked on to have consented, and thereby submitted to any government, where he has made no expressions of it at all."[10] It seems that tacit consent need not really be expressed in the strict sense at all for Locke. Tacit consent can be understood or inferred by the observer, quite independent of the consentor's intentions or awareness that he is consenting. This is borne out by Locke's answer to his question: "And to this I say that every man, that hath any possession, or enjoyment, of any part of the dominions of any government, doth thereby give his tacit consent, and is as far forth obliged to obedience to the laws of that government. . . . "[11]

Now I have already suggested that tacit consent should

not be taken by the consent theorist to be an "unex-
pressed" consent; calling consent tacit on my account
specifies its mode of expression, not its lack of expression.
But this is not the only thing which makes Locke's account of consent seem suspicious. For Locke, owning
land in the state, lodging in a house in the state, traveling
on a highway in the state, all are ways in which one gives
his consent. In fact, signs of consent go "as far as the very
being of any one within the territories of that government."[12] Now, it is important to understand that Locke is
not just saying that these are ways in which one might
give his consent without putting it into words; that, of
course, would be quite unobjectionable since nearly any
act can, given suitable background conditions including
the right sorts of conventions, be one whereby a man expresses his consent. Locke is saying rather that, in modern
states at least, these acts necessarily constitute the giving
of tacit consent. In other words, such acts are always signs
of consent, regardless of the intentions of the actor or his
special circumstances.

It is easy to see that this sort of "consent" violates
(within modern states) nearly all of the general conditions
necessary for an act to be an act of giving consent, tacit or
otherwise. Most importantly, of course, Locke's suggestion that binding consent can be given unintentionally is
a patent absurdity. The weakness of Locke's notion of
consent has even led some to question Locke's traditionally accepted status as a consent theorist (indeed, as
the classic consent theorist). The most interesting feature
of Hanna Pitkin's "Obligation and Consent" is precisely
such a questioning of Locke's devotion to personal consent as the ground of political obligation. I want to summarize her argument briefly, since analyzing it will lead
us, I think, to a consideration of one of the fundamental
confusions about tacit consent that has plagued discussions of this topic.

Pitkin argues that in widening his definition of consent
so as "to make it almost unrecognizable," Locke seems to

make a citizen's consent virtually automatic. "Why," she asks, "all the stress on consent if it is to include everything we do?"[13] Among other things, this forces us to conclude that residence within the territory of the worst sort of tyranny would constitute consent to it, which conclusion seems far indeed from Locke's intentions. But, of course, Locke holds that we cannot become bound to such a government even if we try.[14] How then can he reconcile this position with his claim that residence always constitutes consent? Pitkin answers that Locke intends tacit consent to be understood as a special consent given only to "the terms of the original contract which the founders of the commonwealth made."[15] In this manner, residing in or using roads within the territories of a government that is tyrannical or is otherwise acting ultra vires does not constitute tacit consent to the rule of that government. Only when the government acts within its assigned limits do these acts constitute consent.

Regardless of the merits of this argument as an exercise in Locke scholarship, the conclusion Pitkin draws is an interesting one. She maintains that, insofar as consent is virtually automatic in Locke, Locke did not really take personal consent seriously as a ground of political obligation. Rather, she interprets Locke as holding that "you are obligated to obey because of certain characteristics of the government—that it is acting within the bounds of a trusteeship based on an original contract."[16] Further, since she reads Locke as holding that "the terms of the original contract are . . . self-evident truths," Locke can be understood as claiming that our obligations in fact arise from the government's conformity to the only possible terms of a not necessarily actual (i.e., possibly hypothetical) contract.

The interesting aspect of this conclusion is the way in which it ties Locke to two contemporary methods for approaching these political problems. First, it brings Locke closer to what is often called a theory of "hypothetical contract," whereby the quality of government is determined in reference to the limits which would be placed on it by rational and self-interested original contractors. This sort of theory has its most mature formulation in John Rawls's *A Theory of Justice*. Second, Pitkin makes Locke appear more like contemporary writers who deemphasize individuals' histories in a theory of political obligation, to stress instead the quality of the government as the source from which our political obligations arise.

This reading of Locke is obviously inconsistent with the radical individualism and voluntarism so evident throughout the *Second Treatise*. But my belief that Pitkin's reading is mistaken is based on more than a desire to preserve intact the Lockean spirit. I think that the oddity of Pitkin's interpretation can be explained by pointing to a single mistake which she makes in understanding Locke's position. The mistake is made when Pitkin concludes that the obligation to obey the government must derive from the quality of the government in question. This conclusion is essentially drawn from two sound premises: first, residence for Locke always constitutes consent; and second, for Locke we are bound to obey good governments but not bad ones. Pitkin concludes that consent must be essentially irrelevant to our political bonds in Locke's theory, for it seems inconsistent to hold all of the following: (1) By residing within their territories, we give our consent even to bad governments; (2) we are not obligated to bad governments; and (3) consent is the ground of political obligation. To preserve consistency in Locke, Pitkin sacrifices (3); but she seems to ignore the possibility that consent might be only a necessary, rather than a sufficient, condition for the generation of political obligations. Let me clarify this observation by again describing a parallel case involving promises.

I make two promises to a friend—one to help him commit murder most foul, the other to give him half my yearly income. It is usually maintained, and it is certainly my belief, that while both promises are real promises, the latter obligates me while the former does not. But following reasoning similar to Pitkin's, we ought to conclude from this that the obligation I am under to keep this latter promise arises solely from the morally commendable (or at least not morally prohibited) quality of the promised act. But this conclusion would be false. The obligation arises solely from my having promised. The moral quality of the act merely *prevents* one of the promises (the one to commit murder) from obligating me. But in no way is the morally acceptable quality of the other promised act the *ground* of my obligation to perform it.

Similarly, we might hold that consent to the authority of a tyrannical government does not bind one, just as a promise to act immorally does not bind one. And while I have suggested earlier that I think that consent to a tyranny *can* sometimes bind one, Locke's position, I maintain, is exactly that described above. Locke holds that our consent only binds us when it is given to good governments. But consent is still the sole ground of the obligation. The quality of the government is, for Locke, merely a feature relevant to the binding force of the consent. This he makes quite clear, I think, in Chapter IV: "For a man, not having the power over his own life, cannot, by compact, or his own consent, enslave himself to any one, nor put himself under the absolute, arbitrary power of another. . . . "[17]

Here Locke asserts that while a man may consent to an arbitrary government's rule, he is never bound to that government, for becoming so bound would involve disposing of rights which he does not possess. This suggests to me that Locke's doctrine of personal consent can with perfect consistency be joined to the claims that residence in any state constitutes consent and that we are only bound to good governments. All that is needed is the additional premise that consent is not always sufficient to obligate. In overlooking Locke's use of this premise, Pitkin has been led to misinterpret Locke's account of political obligation, emphasizing the quality of the government over the consensual act.

I do not, of course, deny that in saying that a man who

gives his tacit consent is "as far forth obliged to obedience," Locke appears to make consent sufficient for obligation. I suggest, however, that we understand him here
to be thinking specifically of good governments, or, at
worst, to be suffering from momentary carelessness. For
when he begins seriously to consider tyrannical and arbitrary forms of government later in the *Second Treatise*,
Locke frequently repeats his claim that we cannot bind
ourselves to such governments by any means, compact
included,[18] although we can certainly consent to such
governments. Consent in Locke, then, cannot be sufficient
always to generate obligations.

My suggestion is that we can believe Locke when he asserts that he holds personal consent to be the sole ground
of political obligation. His claims on this point seem to be
consistent, if perhaps mistaken. Still, one cannot help but
be suspicious, as Pitkin certainly was, of a consent theory
in which consent seems to fade into whatever is necessary
to obligate everyone living under a good government.
And these suspicions may again lead us to believe that
Locke was really only halfhearted in his insistence on
personal consent as the source of our political bonds.

I would like to suggest, however, that these suspicions
can be allayed somewhat by understanding Locke as having become muddled about a distinction that has been
similarly missed by many political theorists down to the
present day. That distinction is between acts which are
"signs of consent" and acts which "imply consent." In
calling an act a "sign of consent," I mean that because of
the context in which the act was performed, including the
appropriate conventions (linguistic or otherwise), the act
counts as an expression of the actor's intention to consent;
thus, all genuine consensual acts are the givings of "signs
of consent." But in saying that an act "implies consent,"
we mean neither that the actor intended to consent nor
that the act would normally be taken as an attempt to consent. There are three ways in which an act might be said to
"imply consent" in the sense I have in mind.

1. An act may be such that it leads us to conclude that the actor was in an appropriate frame of mind to, or had attitudes which would lead him to, consent if suitable conditions arose. This conclusion may be expressed by the conditional: if he had been asked to (or if an appropriate situation had otherwise arisen), he would have consented.

2. An act may be such that it "commits" the actor to consenting. By this I mean that the act would be pointless or hopelessly stupid unless the actor was fully prepared to consent; the act commits the actor "rationally" to giving his consent. Thus, for example, discoursing at great length on how a man would be an idiot not to consent to be governed by the government would, under normal circumstances, imply consent to be so governed, in sense 2 (as well, perhaps, as in sense 1).

3. An act may be such that it binds the actor morally to the same performance to which he would be bound if he had in fact consented. I may do something which is not itself an act of consent, but which nonetheless binds me as if I had consented; after performing the act, it would be wrong (ceteris paribus) for me not to do those things which my actual consent would have bound me to do. Consider a simple case like joining a game of baseball. Many writers have held that although in joining the game I do nothing which could be construed as giving my consent (tacit or otherwise) to be governed by the umpire's decisions, nonetheless, by participating in the activity, I may become bound to be so governed, just as I would be if I had in fact consented. The analysis of the ground of this moral bond, however, would appeal to something other than the performance of a deliberate undertaking, focusing instead on, e.g., the receipt of benefits from or the taking advantage of some established scheme.

All of these three are types of acts which I will say "imply consent," though none of them is normally a "sign of consent." Each is closely related to genuine consent in some way without in fact being consent. I believe that in his peculiar notion of tacit consent Locke has actually, but unknowingly, developed a notion of acts which may very well "imply consent" in sense 3. Tacit consent is for Locke, remember, a consent which is not expressed but which is given in the performance of certain acts; in particular, Locke specifies the "enjoyments" of certain benefits granted by the state as being the sorts of acts in which we are interested. These "enjoyments" are seen by Locke to "imply consent" in the sense that it would be morally wrong for us to accept these enjoyments while refusing to accept the government's authority. When we enjoy the public highways, owning land, police protection, etc., our "acts of enjoyment," though not expressions of our consent, nonetheless are thought by Locke to "imply" our consent by binding us to obedience as if we had in fact consented.

This may seem at first a very implausible position, for it appears to make the generation of very important obligations hang on the performance of very unimportant "acts of enjoyment," such as traveling on public highways. But at least this much can be said in Locke's defense—he was clearly aware that the various enjoyments he mentions do not come packaged separately. When one owns land or travels the highways in a state, one does not *just* enjoy those simple benefits. More importantly, one enjoys the benefits of the rule of law, police protection, protection by the armed forces, etc. And because these benefits are unavoidable for anyone within the government's effective domain, Locke recognizes that "the very being of any one within the territories" of the government will serve quite as well as any of the more specific "enjoyments" he mentions; one receives this important package of the benefits of government simply by being within "the parts whereof the force of its law extends."[19] Thus, the political obligations of "tacit consentors" may not arise from such insignificant enjoyments as it might at first have seemed.

But of course my chief purpose here is to examine Locke's *analysis* of this ground of political obligation, and it is in this analysis that the most obvious problems arise. For in his dedication to personal consent as the sole ground of political obligation, Locke confusedly labels the enjoyments of the benefits of government as a special sort of consensual act—"tacit" consent. But we have seen that while Locke's "enjoyments" might "imply consent," and might therefore have "something to do with" personal consent, they are not "signs of consent." Such enjoyments are not normally deliberate undertakings. In trying to rob consent of its intentionality, Locke succeeds only in undermining the appeal of his own consent theory, with its dedication to the thesis that only through deliberate undertakings can we become politically bound.

My suggestion is that none of Locke's "consent-implying enjoyments" is in fact a genuine consensual act. In analyzing any obligations which might arise from such enjoyments, we do not appeal to a principle of consent. Rather, such obligations would arise, if at all, because of considerations of fairness or gratitude. Locke's primary error, then, seems to lie in his confusion of consent with other grounds which may be sufficient to generate obligations, grounds which may at best be called "consent-implying."

But if Locke was confused about this distinction between "signs of consent" and "consent-implying" acts, he is certainly not alone. Political theorists have remained confused on the same point for the nearly three hundred years since Locke's ground-breaking confusion. Over and over it is claimed that voting in an election, running for political office, applying for a passport, etc. are signs of consent to the political institutions of the state which bind the actor accordingly. Alexander Meiklejohn[20] and Alan Gewirth[21] both seem to argue in this way. But perhaps the best contemporary example of this confusion surfaces in the second edition of J. P. Plamenatz's *Consent, Freedom, and Political Obligation*. Plamenatz, after avoiding many of these confusions in the body of his book, observes in his apologetic "Postscript to the Second

Edition" that certian acts "signify" consent without being simple "expressions" of consent.° He is concerned particularly with voting:

> If Smith were in fact elected, it would be odd to say of anyone who had voted for him that he did not consent to his holding office. . . . Where there is an established process of election to an office, then, provided the election is free, anyone who takes part in the process consents to the authority of whoever is elected to the office.[22]

And beyond just voting, people can be properly said to consent to a political system simply "by taking part in its processes."[23]

But if my account of consent has been correct, all of these observations must be mistaken. For while political participation may "imply consent" (or might *under special arrangements* be a sign of consent), it is not under current arrangements in most states a sign of consent. One

---

° In his *Man and Society*, Plamenatz introduces a special terminology to distinguish the two sorts of "consent" he has in mind. "Direct consent" is the sort of consent I have discussed in this chapter, and it can be either tacit or express. But in addition to "direct consent," there is "indirect consent," which is given to a government by voting or abstaining from voting (*Man and Society*, vol. I, 239-241). Introducing a special terminology, however, will not solve the problem (and Plamenatz's arguments in *Man and Society* are no more convincing than the arguments considered below). It has long been popular to defend the most unusual suggestions about "consent" by using modifiers like "tacit," "implicit," "covert," etc. Bentham clearly found the situation amusing when he wrote, in *Truth versus Ashhurst*:

Ashhurst. —Happily for us, we are not bound by any laws but such as are ordained by the virtual consent of the whole kingdom.
Truth.   —Virtual, Mr. Justice?—what does that mean? real or imaginary? . . .
          "Happily for you," said Muley Ishmael once to the people of Morocco, "Happily for you, you are bound by no laws but what have your virtual consent: for they are all made by your virtual representative, and I am he."

In J. Bowring (ed.), *The Works of Jeremy Bentham*, Simpkin, Marshall & Co., 1843, vol. V, p. 235.

may, and probably the average man does, register and
vote with only minimal awareness that one is participating at all, and with no intention whatsoever of consenting
to anything. Talk of consent in such situations can be no
more than metaphorical.[24]

It is easy to be misled, as Plamenatz probably was, by
what I will call the "attitudinal" sense of "consent";
"consent" in this sense is merely having an attitude of
approval or dedication. And certainly it would be odd
(though not inconceivable) if a man who ran for public
office did not "consent" to the political system in this attitudinal sense, or if the man who voted for him did not
"consent" to his holding office. Voting, after all, is normally at least in part a sign of approval. But this sense of
"consent" is quite irrelevant to our present discussion,
where we are concerned exclusively with consent in the
"occurrence" sense, i.e., with consent as an act which
may generate obligations. An attitude of approval or dedication is completely irrelevant to the rights and obligations of the citizen who has it. When a man consents, he
has consented and may be bound accordingly, regardless
of how he feels about what he has consented to. It is my
belief that confusions about this attitudinal-occurrence
distinction, conjoined with similar failures to distinguish
signs of consent from consent-implying acts, are responsible for most of the mistakes made in discussions of consent theory from Locke down to contemporary writers.

All of this has been leading, of course, to the conclusion
that tacit consent must meet the same fate as express consent concerning its suitability as a general ground of political obligation. For it seems clear that very few of us have
ever tacitly consented to the government's authority in
the sense developed in this essay; the situations appropriate for such consent simply do not arise frequently.
Without major alterations in modern political processes
and conventions, consent theory's big gun turns out to be
of woefully small caliber. While consent, be it tacit or express, may still be the firmest ground of political obliga-

tion (in that people who have consented probably have fewer doubts about their obligations than others), it must be admitted that in most modern states consent will only bind the smallest minority of citizens to obedience. Only attempts to expand the notion of tacit consent beyond proper limits will allow consent to appear to be a suitably general ground of political obligation.

And while we have admitted that Locke does attempt such an illegitimate expansion, we can, from another vantage point, see that Locke was not completely confused in this attempt. For Locke's unconscious transition to "consent-implying" acts as grounds of obligation includes the important (though unstated) recognition that deliberate undertakings, such as promises or consensual acts, may *not* be necessary for the generation of political obligations; other sorts of acts may serve as well, in spite of their not being genuine acts of consent. This recognition, however, cannot form a part of a consent theory, with its insistence on consent as the sole ground of political obligation.

But it is nonetheless an important insight. The "enjoyments" of benefits of government (which Locke mistakenly classifies as acts of tacit consenting) may very well generate political obligations, as Locke believed. These obligations would not, however, fall under principles of fidelity or consent. There are, of course, other sorts of obligations than those generated by consent, and Locke seems to rely on them while, as a consent theorist, officially denying their existence. Thus, some of Locke's consent-implying enjoyments might in fact bind us to political communities under a "principle of fair play," as developed by Hart[25] and Rawls;[26] or they might be thought to bind us under a principle of gratitude, as Plamenatz at one point suggests,[27] or under some other kind of principle of repayment. If so, then Locke's intuitions about obligation, and those of more recent consent theorists, may be essentially sound. Their mistakes may lie primarily in confusing obligation-generating acts with consensual acts,[28] and in overlooking the fact that the consent-implying status of an act is substantially irrelevant to the obligation it generates. Consent theory, then, while it surely fails to give a suitably general account of our political obligations, seems to point the way toward other avenues of inquiry which may prove more rewarding. We will turn our attention in Chapter V to one of these "avenues" (the principle of fair play) and in Chapter VII to the other (the principle of gratitude).

IV.iv. Tacit Consent and Residence

I have, to this point, said relatively little about a problem of tacit consent that lies at the heart of most contemporary works in consent theory. This is the problem of "tacit consent through residence." Locke, as we have observed, believed that residence was a sign of tacit consent. Similarly, Rousseau maintains that "when the State is instituted, residence constitutes consent; to dwell within its territory is to submit to the Sovereign."[29] And more recently, W. D. Ross has written that an "implicit promise to obey" is involved in permanent residence in a state.[30] We have, of course, argued that residence cannot reasonably be thought to constitute genuine consent (given, at least, the current state of political conventions). For it to do so, continued residence would have to be (among other things) a lack of response to a clearly presented "choice situation" allowing for consent or dissent. And clearly, no such choice is ever made available to most of us.

But Socrates has "the Laws" tell us in the *Crito* that Athens systematically did present such a "choice situation" to its people:

> We openly proclaim this principle, that any Athenian, on attaining to manhood and seeing for himself the political organization of the state and us its laws, is permitted, if he is not satisfied with us, to take his

property and go away wherever he likes. If any of you chooses to go to one of our colonies, supposing that he should not be satisfied with us and the state, or to emigrate to any other country, not one of the laws hinders or prevents him from going away wherever he likes, without any loss of property. On the other hand, if any one of you stands his ground when he can see how we administer justice and the rest of our public organization, we hold that by doing so he has in fact undertaken to do anything that we tell him.[31]

Socrates, in this remarkably modern dialogue, develops a claim of tacit consent through residence which is much more plausible than the Locke-Rousseau conception (which does not have the benefit of such a choice situation). Our question becomes, then, is it possible through suitable alterations in our political processes to make residence a genuine sign of tacit consent? The answer to this question should be of great importance to contemporary consent theorists like Joseph Tussman and Michael Walzer; for obviously, if one believes that consent is the only ground of political obligation, and that a government's legitimacy depends on the consent of its citizens, then the very possibility of legitimate government and widespread political obligation will turn on the possibility of instituting such a choice situation, to draw out the consent of the masses. But there are also other reasons for believing that a situation in which residence constituted consent would be a desirable one. For in that case, each citizen would know that he had consented to the government's authority, and one aspect of his doubts about how he ought to behave in matters political would be eliminated. Further, not only might the presentation of a choice situation heighten awareness of membership in a community, but presumably a general knowledge that such awareness was shared by one's fellow citizens would reap further benefits of trust and cooperation.

I mention these points only to emphasize the fact that

the possibility of making residence a genuine sign of consent is not an idle issue. Now one very well-known argument concludes that mere residence could never be a sign of consent, and this conclusion presumably applies even to states which *do* formalize a choice between residence and emigration. This argument was first suggested by Hume, and has been used frequently since that time.[32] The argument runs as follows: residence can never constitute tacit consent to the government's rule, because it is always possible for self-professed revolutionaries, spies, anarchists, gangsters, and outlaws to reside within a state. But to suggest that such men consent, even tacitly, to the rule of a government they actively oppose seems ludicrous.

As popular as this argument has been, it seems to me to be obviously not to the point. Why exactly does it seem ludicrous that an outlaw should be thought to consent to the government? Presumably, it is because he actively works against and clearly disapproves of the government. But if this is the reason, then the argument makes consent into an attitude rather than an act. That this is so can be seen in the fact that even if an outlaw *had* consented, it would seem just as odd to say that he consents to the government. The force of the argument derives from the apparent assumption that one who opposes the government cannot possibly have consented to it, no matter what he has done. But this assumption is clearly false. While it may be true that outlaws and spies do not "consent" in the "attitudinal sense" mentioned earlier (IV.iii), such "attitudinal consent" is irrelevant to the problems of political obligation and genuine consent. And even if the argument were that an outlaw would never, in a sane moment, consent (in the occurrence sense) *sincerely*, it could succeed only if we saw sincerity as essential to the success of an act of consent. But, of course, just as we can make binding promises with no intention of keeping them, we can perfectly well consent with no intention of allowing the exercise of the right we accord to another in consenting. The existence of outlaws, then, does not seem to endanger the attempt to show that residence could constitute consent, given suitable alterations in political conventions. For we must remember that in discussing the relation of consent to political obligation we are concerned only with the occurrence sense of consent.

We can, then, return to our original question: could a formal choice situation, like the one described by Socrates, make continued residence a sign of consent? Joseph Tussman has answered this question in the affirmative. As long as the situation makes it clear that one who remains a resident is aware of the significance of so remaining, and as long as there remains a genuine alternative to giving one's tacit consent, then residence will be a sign of consent. We should not be concerned, Tussman argues, that the alternative to consent, namely emigration, is such an unpleasant alternative.[33] For "to say that consenting to the status of a member is involuntary because the alternative is not as pleasant or convenient is simply to confuse convenience with necessity"; the unpleasantness of emigration "does not rob a deliberate choice of its voluntary character."[34]

A formal choice procedure, then, seems to satisfy the demands that consent be knowingly given and voluntary. Similarly, such a procedure could easily be structured to satisfy our first three conditions for giving consent through silence—a clear choice situation, a period where dissent is invited, and a limit to time for allowable dissent. But it is not so clear that our conditions 4 and 5 will be satisfied by such a procedure. These conditions state that silence or inactivity cannot be taken as a sign of consent if the means of indicating dissent are unreasonable or very difficult to perform or if the consequences of dissent are extremely detrimental to the consentor. Emigration is a difficult course which might well have disastrous consequences. Of course, even if conditions 4 and 5 were not met, we might still want to call the act of remaining in residence a "voluntary act"; but it is not clear that mere voluntariness is sufficient to make such an act a sign of consent, as Tussman apparently believes. One cannot but feel somewhat inclined to agree with Hume on this point:

> Can we seriously say, that a poor peasant or partizan has a free choice to leave his country, when he knows no foreign language or manners, and lives from day to day, by the small wages which he acquires. We may as well assert that a man, by remaining in a vessel, freely consents to the dominion of the master; though he was carried on board while asleep, and must leap into the ocean, and perish, the moment he leaves her.[35]

Does a man choose freely to remain in prison because he has a knife with which he can wound himself seriously enough to be removed to a hospital? These are strong metaphors, but it is easy to respond that our choice procedure can make provisions for dealing with such difficult cases. It might include, for instance, provisions for assisting the poor and oppressed (who would most desire and be least able to leave) in emigrating.

Would these sorts of provisions finally render continued residence a sign of tacit consent? There is one other problem which suggests that even with such provisions our choice procedure could not satisfy conditions 4 and 5 for tacit consent; and this problem cannot be circumvented by simply adding new provisions to the choice procedure. The problem is that it is precisely the most valuable "possessions" a man has that are often tied necessarily to his country of residence and cannot be taken from it. Most men will treasure home, family, and friends above all things. But these goods are not moveable property and cannot simply be packed on the boat with one's books and television set. Even if a man's home is in a tyrannical state, home can still be the most important thing in his life. And this places a very heavy weight on the side of continued residence. Emigration cannot be thought of as merely unpleasant or inconvenient for most of us; it may very well constitute a "disaster," if only a small one. And if that is true, it may well be that emigration routinely has consequences sufficiently unpleasant to make any formal political choice procedures fail our condition 5. In that case, we would be justified in concluding that no such procedure could ever allow us to take continued residence as a sign of tacit consent to the government's authority. The challenge, then, seems to remain open to the modern-day consent theorist to show us how government by consent can be made a reality. In any event, however, the more plausible alternative is to turn our attention from consent to other possible grounds of political obligation.

CHAPTER V

The Principle of Fair Play

V.i. Hart and Rawls on Fair Play

In Chapter IV, we saw how many consent theorists have recognized as grounds of political obligation acts which are not consensual acts, promises, or contracts. Primarily through utilizing what I called "consent-implying" acts, Locke and other consent theorists confusedly, and unintentionally, acknowledged the existence of grounds of political obligation which were not deliberate undertakings. These grounds were acts which seemed to bind the individual to the state, and seemed to be related to consent in some way; they were recognized as morally significant acts, but were mistakenly subsumed under the title of consent. Specifically, the "consent-implying" acts in question were the "enjoyments" of the benefits of government within the state.

The problem, then, has become one of understanding the significance of these sorts of acts in new (i.e., not consent-related) terms. If we allow that these acts, which are not consensual in character, may nonetheless generate political obligations, how are we to explain this possibility? One sort of explanation which has enjoyed some popularity during the last two decades relies on what has been called "the Principle of Fair Play"[1] (or "the Principle of Fairness"). I suggested in Chapter IV that this principle might be regarded in some ways as an extension of certain consent theory intuitions; but more often, it is regarded as simply a replacement for consent theory. H.L.A. Hart, for instance, in the first concise formulation of the principle of fair play, writes:

> A third important source of special rights and obligations which we recognize in many spheres of life is

what may be termed mutuality of restrictions, and I think political obligation is intelligible only if we see what precisely this is and how it differs from the other right-creating transactions (consent, promising) to which philosophers have assimilated it.[2]

Hart's comments on the principle (and on its application to political cases) are fairly sparse, but I want to examine them briefly by way of introduction. Hart's explanation of the "special transaction" he has in mind runs as follows:

> When a number of persons conduct any joint enterprise according to rules and thus restrict their liberty, those who have submitted to these restrictions when required have a right to a similar submission from those who have benefited by their submission. The rules may provide that officials should have authority to enforce obedience . . . but the moral obligation to obey the rules in such circumstances is due to the cooperating members of the society, and they have the correlative moral right to obedience.[3]

While Hart does not refer to this source of special rights and obligations in terms of fairness or fair play, he does note later that "in the case of mutual restrictions we are in fact saying that this claim to interfere with another's freedom is justified because it is fair."[4] We can understand him, then, to be claiming that in the situation described, a beneficiary has an obligation to "do his fair share" by submitting to the rules when they require it; others who have cooperated before have a right to this fair distribution of the burdens of submission.

Clearly, Hart intends to restrict the generation of rights and obligations under the principle of fair play to certain special contexts. Not just any situation in which we would be inclined to talk of fair play will suffice. The salient features of these special contexts seem to be: 1) a number of individuals participate in an "enterprise"; 2) a set of rules (according to which individuals are uniformly restricted in their actions) governs the enterprise; 3) when some (or all) of the participants follow the rules, certain benefits accrue to some (or all) of the participants—but these benefits may be gotten in at least some cases without following the rules when one's turn comes. Under these conditions, when a person (who must presumably be a participant, although Hart does not specify this) benefits from others having followed the rules, he has an "obligation of fair play" also to follow the rules, and those who have followed the rules have a right to his cooperation.

A large number of questions concerning this account come immediately to the fore. What is to be counted as "an enterprise"? (Will any "project" be "an enterprise"? Must participants be "members," or have joined in some way?) Why is a set of rules necessary? (Mightn't a principle of fair play apply as well to nonrule-governed enterprises?) How do we specify the class of beneficiaries to whom obligations are ascribed? (Who counts as a participant, and who as an "outsider"?) Must a "fair share" of benefits be received to obligate the recipient to do his "fair share" in following the rules? The list can go on. Obviously, Hart's account leaves out far more than it fills in (but in fairness, it was not intended as a complete account—Hart's essay does not profess to give this principle any more than a superficial treatment). What is needed for our present purposes is a fuller discussion of both the principle itself and its application to political cases.

Both needs are best met by John Rawls's 1964 essay, "Legal Obligation and the Duty of Fair Play." In it Rawls builds on Hart's account to give both a more complete account of the principle of fair play and an extensive discussion of its application to constitutional democracies. (Rawls's later account of the principle in A Theory of Justice is substantially the same; in many respects, however, the account presently under discussion is more detailed and hence more suitable for present purposes.)[5] The ways in which Rawls elaborates on and adds to Hart's principle are, I think, interesting. Rawls's central presentation of the principle of fair play runs:

> The principle of fair play may be defined as follows. Suppose there is a mutually beneficial and just scheme of social cooperation, and that the advantages it yields can only be obtained if everyone, or nearly everyone, cooperates. Suppose further that cooperation requires a certain sacrifice from each person, or at least involves a certain restriction of his liberty. Suppose finally that the benefits produced by cooperation are, up to a certain point, free: that is, the scheme of cooperation is unstable in the sense that if any one person knows that all (or nearly all) of the others will continue to do their part, he will still be able to share a gain from the scheme even if he does not do his part. Under these conditions a person who has accepted the benefits of the scheme is bound by a duty of fair play to do his part and not to take advantage of the free benefits by not cooperating.[6]

The context within which obligations (or duties— Rawls is not particularly concerned here with the distinction between them) of fair play can arise, as described by Rawls, can be seen to exhibit three important features parallel to those we discerned in Hart's account:

1. There must be an active scheme of social cooperation. This does not really advance us much beyond Hart's "enterprise," but I think that both writers clearly intended that the principle cover a broad range of schemes, programs, enterprises, etc., differing in size and in significance. Thus, a tenant organization's program to improve conditions in their apartment building, and an entire political community's cooperative efforts to preserve social order, both seem to qualify as "enterprises" or "schemes of social cooperation" of the appropriate sort. Rawls does set two explicit conditions, however, which

help us limit the class of "schemes" he has in mind. First, they must be "mutually beneficial." This condition is, I think, implicit in Hart's account as well; indeed, the principle would be obviously objectionable in its absence. Second, the schemes must be just. This condition is nowhere alluded to by Hart, and I will consider it carefully in V.ii. In his later discussions of the principle (see note 5), Rawls introduces the term "institution" to replace "scheme of social cooperation." I find this term not only equally nebulous, but unnecessarily restrictive. Surely fair play considerations apply to many schemes which do not involve anything we would want to call an "institution." When nine friends decide to collect newspapers from neighbors to sell as scrap, in order to raise money for their softball team, their scheme hardly seems to constitute an "institution" (at the very least, we would say that this seems too "formal" a title). Yet when one of the nine plays on the team while failing to help in the collections, surely our criticism would be made in terms of "fair play."

2. Cooperation under the scheme involves at least a restriction of one's liberty. Rawls does not mention here, as Hart does, that this restriction be in accord with a system of rules which govern the scheme by determining the requirements of cooperation (although his later "institutional" language does follow Hart's requirement). Frankly, I can see no good reason to insist on the rule-governedness of the enterprise. Might not an enterprise be of the right sort which, say, assigned burdens fairly but not in accord with any preestablished rules? Cannot doing one's part be obligatory under considerations of fair play even if "one's part" is not rule-specified? Consider again the example of the paper collection. Must there be a set of rules which specifies the part which each participant must play in the collection? It seems that it would be obligatory for each to do "his part" in the scheme, even if that "part" is not clearly defined by rules. But perhaps my

objection simply involves a stricter reading of "system of rules" than either Hart or Rawls has in mind.

3. The benefits yielded by the scheme may be gotten in at least some cases by someone who does not cooperate when his turn comes; here Rawls again makes explicit a condition which Hart clearly has in mind (since "free riding" is a problem only when this condition obtains). But Rawls adds to this the condition that the benefits in question can be obtained only if nearly all of the participants cooperate. I confess that I again do not see the necessity of this condition. Would it be any less unfair to take the benefits of the cooperative sacrifices of others if those benefits could be obtained even if one-third or one half of the participants neglected their responsibilities toward the scheme? Would this make that neglect justifiable? Surely not. A scheme which requires uniform cooperation when only 50 percent cooperation is needed may perhaps be an inefficient scheme; but it is not clear that this would make considerations of fair play inapplicable. Consider a community scheme to preserve water pressure which prohibits watering lawns in the evening, when in fact if half of the members watered their lawns there would be no lowering of water pressure. Surely this is an inefficient plan, compared to alternatives. But once the plan was instituted, would a member be any more justified in watering his lawn in the evening than if only a few people's so doing would lower the water pressure? I think it is clear that he would not be. Certainly free riding is more dangerous to the scheme's successful provision of benefits when Rawls's requirement obtains; it may then be even more objectionable in those cases. But this additional objectionable element seems to have nothing to do with considerations of *fair play*.[p]

[p] This argument also seems to me to provide an effective response to a recent attack on the principle of fair play made by M.B.E. Smith (in "Is There a Prima Facie Obligation to Obey the Law?"). Smith argues that failing to cooperate in a scheme after receiving benefits is only unfair if by this failure we deny someone else benefits within the scheme. But my

Rawls's account, then, seems to conform to either the letter or the spirit of Hart's account fairly consistently. One significant addition Rawls makes, however, is to move beyond Hart's simple requirement that an individual have benefited from the scheme in order to become bound. Rawls specifies that the obligation depends on "our having accepted and our intention to continue accepting the benefits of a just scheme of cooperation. . . ."[7] We have, then, a move from mere benefaction in Hart's case, to a positive *acceptance* of benefits in Rawls's account. (The "intention to continue accepting benefits" seems quite beside the point here, and Rawls drops that clause in later versions; I will ignore it.) While the distinction between benefiting and accepting benefits is usually not easy to draw in actual cases, that there is such a distinction, and that it is of great significance to moral questions, is undeniable. Suppose that I am kidnapped by a mad doctor and dragged to his laboratory, where he forces on me an injection of an experimental drug. When I discover that the result of the injection is a great increase in my intelligence and strength, it is undeniable that I have benefited from the injection; but it would be a simple abuse of language to say that I had "accepted" the benefits which I received. Or consider the difference between the cases in which a stranger (a) sneaks into my yard while I am out of town and mows my lawn, and (b) asks me if I'd like to have my lawn mowed, and proceeds to mow it after receiving an affirmative response. In both cases I have clearly received a benefit (in fact, the same benefit), but

example is precisely a case in which the failure to cooperate may not deny anyone else benefits within the scheme. And still it looks as if failure to cooperate is unfair, for by failing to do his part, the individual *takes advantage* of the others, who act in good faith. Whether or not my cooperation is necessary for benefiting other members, it is not fair for me, as a participant in the scheme, to decide not to do my part when the others do theirs. For these reasons, Smith's argument is unpersuasive, as is J. R. Pennock's similar position in "The Obligation to Obey the Law and the Ends of the State," in S. Hook (ed.), *Law and Philosophy*, New York University Press, 1964.

only in the latter would we say that I had "accepted" that benefit. It seems clear from these examples that we can distinguish, at least in some cases, between mere receipt and positive acceptance of benefits. And it seems equally clear that this distinction may play a crucial role in determining whether or what obligations arise from my having benefited from another's actions.

To have accepted a benefit in the right sense, I must have wanted that benefit when I received it, or have made some effort to get the benefit, or at least not have actively attempted to avoid getting it. I will try to be more precise about this distinction later; here I want only to suggest that Rawls apparently does not see mere benefaction as sufficient to generate an obligation of fair play. He stresses instead the necessity that the benefits be voluntarily accepted by the beneficiary.

This restriction of the principle, of course, seems quite intuitive, for it seems to place us less at the mercy of the whims of cooperative schemes (see my criticism of Nozick's arguments in V.iv). And while I have suggested that Rawls has added to Hart's account in imposing this restriction, once again it is possible that such a restriction was intended by Hart. For he does note that "not all obligations to other persons are deliberately incurred, though I think it is true of all special rights that they arise from previous voluntary actions."[8] In other words, while obligations of fair play need not be deliberately incurred, a voluntary action is required. And what is this voluntary action? It is possible that Hart refers simply to the voluntary act of joining the cooperative scheme. But it is also possible that the voluntary act Hart has in mind as a necessary condition for the generation of obligations of fair play is the voluntary acceptance of benefits from the scheme. Since mere receipt of benefits need not involve any voluntary act, Hart may then have in mind the same sort of restriction on the principle as Rawls. At any rate, the problems associated with this distinction will receive fuller consideration in V.iv and V.v.

V.ii. Fair Play and Justice

Before continuing, however, I want to return to consider briefly one of Rawls's conditions for the generation of obligations of fair play: the condition states that only when the scheme or institution in question is just can any obligations of fair play (relative to that scheme) arise. This claim is part of a more general thesis that we can never be bound to support or comply with unjust arrangements; although Rawls never advances this general thesis in so many words, it follows from his (unacceptable) claim that *all* obligations are accounted for by the principle of fair play,[9] conjoined with the absence of any natural duties which could account for such a bond. It will be recalled, no doubt, that I argued earlier (IV.i) that Rawls was mistaken in his claim that consent to an unjust institution could not bind. It remains now to be asked if the principle of fair play can be limited in application to contexts of just cooperative schemes.[q] An answer to this question is, of course, of some importance, since Rawls's condition would limit significantly the principle's application in both political and nonpolitical settings.

Rawls's requirement that the scheme of cooperation be just is put forward quite casually in the paper we have been considering; although he calls it an "essential condition," as far as I can see, he offers no defense of this claim. Even in the more recent statement of this requirement in *A Theory of Justice*, we are given little in the way of a justification of it. While he suggests that the condition is necessary to guarantee the requisite "background conditions" for obligation,[10] he elaborates on this point only by using the bad argument discussed previously in IV.i, which concerns the fact that "extorted promises are void ab initio." As I argued in the case of consent, of course, the injustice of an institution (or cooperative scheme)

[q] Here considering the principle of fair play only as one of several principles of obligation (i.e., one which does not account for obligations of fidelity and consent, as it does on Rawls's view).

need not have any effect on the voluntariness of my membership in or acceptance of benefits from that scheme. And since it is a failure in terms of voluntariness that renders extorted promises nonbinding, Rawls's argument appears to be a non sequitur in the case of fair play, as well as consent.

As Rawls supplies us with no real arguments for this "justice condition," let us try to construct some for him. Two sorts of arguments suggest themselves as defenses of this condition; the first concerns the purpose of the scheme or the ends it promotes, while the second concerns more directly distribution within the scheme. Our first argument would run as follows: we cannot have obligations to do the morally impermissible, or to support schemes whose purposes are immoral or which promote immoral ends. Since unjust schemes fall within this category, we cannot have an obligation to cooperate within unjust schemes. Now, there are a number of obvious problems with this defense of Rawls's "justice condition." Some of these were discussed earlier when I defended the possibility of binding consent being given to unjust institutions (IV.i). But another problem is this: why does Rawls only disqualify *unjust* schemes, rather than all schemes which promote or aim at *immoral* ends? Why does Rawls not include the more general prohibition?

The reason is, I think, that while these immoral ends of the scheme provide us with a reason for working against it, the justice condition is meant to be tied to the principle in a more intimate fashion. But what is this fashion? Thus far, nothing we have said about fair play seems to have anything to do with the moral status of the scheme's purposes. The intuitive force of the principle of fair play seems to be preserved even for, e.g., criminal conspiracies. The special rights and obligations which arise under the principle are thought to do so because of the special relationships which exist between the cooperating participants; a fair share of the burdens is thought to be owed by a benefiting participant simply because others have sac-

rificed to allow him to benefit within a cooperative
scheme. No reference is made here to the morally acceptable status of the scheme. Simple intuitions about fair
play, then, do not seem to provide a reason for disqualifying unjust cooperative schemes. Rather, they suggest that
obligations of fair play can, at least sometimes, arise within such schemes.

But perhaps another sort of support can be given to
Rawls's condition. This second argument concerns distribution within the scheme, and it certainly has the Rawlsian flavor. We suggest, first, that what the justice condition does is, in effect, amend the principle to read that a
person is bound to do his fair share in supporting a
cooperative scheme only if he has been allocated a fair
share of the benefits of the scheme. Previously, the principle of fair play required only that the individual have accepted benefits from the scheme in order to be bound,
where now it requires that he have accepted benefits *and*
have been allocated at least a fair share of benefits. The
role of the justice condition now appears to be important
and an intimate feature of our intuitions about fair play.
For if a scheme is just, each participant will be allocated a
fair share of the benefits of cooperation; thus, anyone who
benefits from the scheme at all, has the opportunity to
benefit to the extent of a fair share (although he may *accept* less than this). We are guaranteed that the principle
of fair play will apply only to individuals who have been
fairly treated. Our feeling that a person ought not to have
to share equally in supporting a scheme that treats him
unfairly is given voice in this condition. The justice condition, then, on this argument, serves the purpose of as-
suring that a man is bound to do his fair share only if he is
allocated a fair share of benefits (and *accepts* some of
them).

I think that this is an important feature of our intuitions
about fair play, and it also seems a natural way of reading
Rawls. In fact, this may be the argument that Rawls is
suggesting when, in elaborating on the principle, he

notes that if the scheme is just, "each person receives a fair share when all (himself included) do their part."[11] (Rawls's observation is, strictly speaking, false; the justice of a scheme does not guarantee that each person either receives or accepts a fair share.) But if this is the argument Rawls intends for his justice condition, there are serious difficulties for it to overcome. The motivation for including the requirement is (on this reading) to guarantee that an individual not become bound to carry a fair share of the burdens of a cooperative scheme if he has been allocated less than a fair share of its benefits; it is unfair to demand full cooperation from one to whom full benefits are denied. But if this is our reason for including the justice condition, we have surely included too much. Why should we think that the whole scheme must be just for this sort of intuition to be given play? Rawls's justice condition requires that *everyone* be allocated a fair share of benefits if *anyone* is to be bound by an obligation of fair play. But the reasons we have given for including this condition seem only to require that for a particular individual to be bound, *he* must be allocated a fair share. This says nothing about the allocation of benefits in general, or about what benefits *others* are allocated. If some individuals within an unjust scheme are allocated less than a fair share of benefits, then our reasons would support the view that *they* are not bound to carry a fair share of the burdens. But nothing said yet about feelings of fair play seems to exempt from obligation those individuals to whom a fair share of benefits is in fact allocated within an *unjust* scheme. So again the point of Rawls's justice condition comes into doubt.

These arguments may prompt us to think more about the notion of a "fair share" of the burdens of cooperation. For if we understand by this phrase a share of the total burden proportionate to the share of the total benefits allocated to the individual, then we may have no problem in accepting that anyone who accepts *any* benefits from a cooperative scheme is bound to do his "fair share." Our belief that only an individual who is allocated a fair share of the benefits is bound to cooperate may be false. For it seems eminently fair to hold that each is bound to cooperate to the extent that he is allowed to benefit from a cooperative scheme; thus, those who are allocated the largest shares of benefits owe the largest share of burdens. But even one who is allocated a very small share of the benefits is bound to carry a small share of the burdens (provided he accepts the benefits).

Now, it is clear that these intuitions cannot be given full play in the case of schemes whose burdens cannot be unequally distributed. But there may seem to be other difficulties involved in the interpretation of the fair play principle sketched above. First, it seems to entail that the better off are bound to support unjust schemes which favor them, and the more discriminatory the scheme, the more strongly they must support it. And second, it seems to entail that those who are allocated tiny, unfair shares of the benefits are still bound to cooperate with the unjust scheme which mistreats them. These may again seem to be good reasons to limit the principle's application to just schemes. I think this appearance is misleading. First, the principle under discussion does not entail that the better off must support unjust schemes which favor them. While it does specify that they are obligated to repay by cooperation the sacrifices made in their behalf by the other members, the injustice of the scheme is a strong reason for opposing it, and a reason which gains in strength with the degree of injustice. Thus, there are moral considerations which may override the obligations of fair play (depending, of course, on the degree of the injustice of the scheme, among other things). And if we think of the burdens as sacrifices to be made, it seems only fair that the unjustly favored should be heavily burdened. As for the apparent result that the unjustly treated are still bound to support the scheme (even if to a lesser degree) which discriminates against them, this result can also be seen to be mistaken. For if we remember that benefits must be *accepted* in order for an individual to be bound under the principle, the unfairly treated have the option of refusing to accept benefits, hence sparing themselves the obligation to support a scheme which treats them unfairly (and they have, as well, the duty to oppose such unjust schemes, regardless of what obligations they are under). The idea, then, is that only if they willingly accept the benefits of the scheme are participants bound to bear the burdens of cooperation, and only then in proportion to the benefits allocated to them.

I am not sure just how much of the Hart-Rawls conception of the principle of fair play this analysis captures. But the considerations raised above seem to me to be good reasons for rejecting Rawls's "justice condition." While we can, of course, agree with Rawls that intolerably unjust schemes ought not to be furthered (and ought, in fact, to be opposed), there is no logical difficulty, at least, in holding that we may sometimes have obligations of fair play to cooperate within unjust schemes. And the arguments suggest that there may be no nonlogical difficulties either.

V.iii. Fair Play and Political Obligation

To this point we have given a sketchy analysis of various aspects of the principle of fair play and the contexts within which it is supposed to apply. In V.iv I will consider in more detail how defensible the principle will be when applied to actual cases, and in V.v, when applied specifically to political cases. Here I want to pause to consider the way in which the principle of fair play is supposed to yield an account of political obligation, and the changes which this new account introduces into our conception of that obligation.

In the Introduction we observed that each of the different accounts of the ground of political obligation would involve its own special conception of the content of the obligation, as well as the obligee to whom the obligation is owed. The move from consent theory's account to an account utilizing the principle of fair play illustrates this point. On the consent theory account, remember, the ground of the obligation is some deliberate consensual act, promise, or contract; this account entails that both the content of the obligation and the identity of the obligee are dependent on the specific nature of the act performed (and on the context within which it is performed). Thus, the content is determined by determining what is consented to, promised, etc., and the obligee is identified as simply the other party involved in the transaction. On the other hand, an account of political obligation using the principle of fair play (like Hart's) departs from this analysis in significant ways. The specific features of the act which is the ground of the obligation are far less central to a determination of the content of the obligation. For here the ground in question is simply any acceptance of benefits provided through the sacrifices of other participants in a cooperative scheme; the content is, for any such case, doing one's part within the scheme. And the obligee, on the fair play account, is the class of participants in the scheme in question (with the exception of the obligor).

This is not to say, of course, that there are not important continuities between the consent theory account of political obligation and the account using the principle of fair play. Both are "obligation-centered" accounts,[r] and as such both stress the essential voluntariness of the generation of the obligation. On both accounts, a voluntary act is the ground of our political bonds, although the consent theorist insists on the need for a deliberate undertaking where the "fair play theorist" does not. And of course, the fact that the acceptance of benefits may often be what I

---

[r] By an "obligation-centered" account I mean simply an account according to which most or all of the people bound by political bonds, are bound by obligations (in the strict sense of "obligation" explained in I.ii). "Obligation-centered" accounts are to be opposed, of course, to "duty-centered" accounts, according to which most or all of those bound are bound by duties.

have called a "consent-implying act" further illustrates this continuity. But this continuity is not to be mistaken for a sign of identity between the two accounts; both Hart and Rawls are quite clear that the principle of fair play is not just a special principle of consent. Nonetheless, John Ladd, for instance, has interpreted the principle in this way. In commenting on Rawls's "Legal Obligation and the Duty of Fair Play," Ladd notes that "it provides us with a model of consent through participation rather than through contract."[12] I have already argued sufficiently against this sort of error in Chapter IV; it is just one more example of the more than frequent confusion in contemporary literature between what I have called acts which are "signs of consent" and acts which merely "imply consent."

I have already suggested several ways in which the "fair play account" (as I shall hereafter call it) of political obligation alters the way we see the ground, the content, and the obligee for the obligation in question. But I have not yet mentioned the advantages which this account is supposed by its advocates to have over the more traditional account offered by consent theory. Neither, unfortunately, have its advocates. It is, however, fairly easy to guess what advantages one might believe the fair play account to have. First, this account involves viewing political communities in a different way than consent theory; specifically, they are viewed as "communities" in a fairly strict sense. We are to understand political communities as being fundamentally, or at least in part, cooperative enterprises on a very large scale. Citizens thus are thought to stand in a cooperative relationship to their fellows, rather than in an adversary relationship with the government. And this former view may seem to some more realistic than the latter.

But clearly the major advantage which the fair play account of political obligation is thought by its advocates to have, is that it provides a *general* account of our political bonds. No deliberate undertaking is necessary to become obligated under the principle of fair play. One can become bound without trying to and without knowing that one is performing an act which generates an obligation.[13] Since mere acceptance of benefits within the right context generates the obligation, one who accepts benefits within the right context can become bound unknowingly. This is an important difference from consent theory's account, which stressed the necessity of a deliberate undertaking. Thus, while one can neither consent nor accept benefits (in the right sense) unintentionally, one can accept benefits without being aware of the moral consequences of so doing (while being unaware of the moral consequences of consenting defeats the claim that consent was given). The significance of this difference, of course, lies in the possibility of giving a *general* account of political obligation in the two cases. Consent theory's failure to give a general account stemmed from the lack of citizens in modern states who had voluntarily undertaken political obligations in the sense required. At least initially, however, it seems much more plausible to suggest that most or all of us have accepted benefits, as is required to be bound under the principle of fair play. Thus, the possibility of giving a general account using this principle seems to be vastly increased over one which uses a principle of consent. This would *not* be the case, however, if accepting benefits in the right sense required having an understanding of the moral consequences of such acceptance, for certainly most citizens who receive the benefits of government do not have such an understanding.

Exactly what "accepting the benefits of government" amounts to, of course, is not yet entirely clear. Neither is the identity of the "cooperative scheme" embodied in political communities. These points will be discussed as we continue. My aim here has been simply to mention what might seem to be advantages of the fair play account; whether these "advantages" are genuine remains to be seen. But regardless of the advantages this account may have over the consent theory account, it surely falls short of this latter account on one score. Consent is a *clear* ground of obligation. If we are agreed on anything concerning moral requirements, it is that promising and consenting generate them. In specifying a different ground of obligation, the account using the principle of fair play draws away from the paradigm of obligation-generating acts. And to those who are strongly wedded to this paradigm of consent, like Robert Nozick, the principle of fair play may seem a sham.

V.iv. Nozick's Arguments

In Chapter 5 of *Anarchy, State, and Utopia*,[14] Nozick argues against accepting the principle of fair play as a valid moral principle, not just in political settings, but in any settings whatsoever. While he seems to rely more on the snowball effect of deviously arranged examples than on argument, Nozick nonetheless makes a persuasive case against the principle. I will consider Nozick's presentation centrally in the remainder of my examination of the principle, in that it seems to touch at least briefly on most of the problems we will want to discuss.

Nozick begins by describing a cooperative scheme of the sort he thinks Hart and Rawls have in mind, and then suggests that benefaction within that scheme may *not* bind one to do one's part:

> Suppose some of the people in your neighborhood (there are 364 other adults) have found a public address system and decide to institute a system of public entertainment. They post a list of names, one for each day, yours among them. On his assigned day (one can easily switch days) a person is to run the public address system, play records over it, give news bulletins, tell amusing stories he has heard, and so on. After 138 days on which each person has done his part, your day arrives. Are you obligated to take your

turn? You *have* benefited from it, occasionally opening your window to listen, enjoying some music or
chuckling at someone's funny story. The other people
have put themselves out. But must you answer the
call when it is your turn to do so? As it stands, surely
not. Though you benefit from the arrangement, you
may know all along that 364 days of entertainment
supplied by others will not be worth your giving up
one day. You would rather not have any of it and not
give up a day than have it all and spend one of your
days at it. Given these preferences, how can it be that
you are required to participate when your scheduled
time comes?[15]

On the basis of this example and others, Nozick concludes
that we are never bound to cooperate in such contexts (unless we have given our consent to be constrained by the
rules of the cooperative scheme).

Now Nozick does not, to be fair, simply pick the
weakest form of the principle of fair play and then reject it
for its inadequacy in hard cases; he has, in fact, a suggestion for improving the principle in response to the cases
he describes. Having noticed, I suppose, that the case described above favors his conclusions largely because of
the negligible value of the benefits received (can we even
imagine the day-long efforts of our painfully dull neighbors to entertain us as a benefit?), Nozick suggests that "at
the very least one wants to build into the principle of fairness the condition that the benefits to a person from the
actions of others are greater than the cost to him of doing
his share."[16] There is certainly something right about this;
something like this must be built into the idea of a *useful*
cooperative scheme. On the other hand, we can imagine a
defender of the principle saying, "if you weren't prepared
to do your part you oughtn't to have taken *any* benefits
from the scheme, no matter how insignificant." Nozick, of
course, has more to say on this point, and so do I.

Even if we do modify the principle with this condition,

however, Nozick has other arguments against it: "The benefits might only barely be worth the costs to you of doing your share, yet others might benefit from *this* institution much more than you do; they all treasure listening to the public broadcasts. As the person least benefited by the practice, are you obligated to do an equal amount for it?"[17] The understood answer is "No," but we might agree with this answer without agreeing that it tells against the principle. For if we understand by "doing one's part" or "doing one's fair share" not necessarily "doing an equal part," but rather "doing a part proportionate to the part of the benefits received," then the one who benefits least from a cooperative scheme will not be bound to share equally in the burdens of cooperation. I argued for this interpretation in V.ii, and if we accept it, Nozick's PA system example may no longer seem so troublesome. For mightn't we be willing to admit that the individual in question, because he benefited so little, was bound to cooperate, but not to the same extent as others who benefit more from the scheme? Would being obligated to do one's part in the PA scheme seem quite so objectionable if one's part was only, say, an hour's worth of broadcasting, as opposed to the PA enthusiasts', whose parts were one and a half days of broadcasting? There are, perhaps, not clear answers to these questions, and certainly the "too-available" character of the benefits causes some difficulties here (these problems will surface again later).

But surely the defender of the principle of fair play will have more fundamental objections to Nozick's case than these. In the first place, the individual in Nozick's PA example does not seem to be a *participant* in the scheme in the sense that Hart and Rawls may have in mind. While he does live in the neighborhood within which the scheme operates, and he does benefit from it, he is still very much of an "innocent bystander." The PA system scheme has been built up around him in such a way that he could not escape its influence. And, of course, the whole force of Nozick's example lies in our feeling that others should not be able to *force* any scheme they like upon us, with the attendant obligations. The PA case would be precisely such a case of "forced" obligation. So naturally we may find Nozick's criticism of the principle of fair play convincing, if we believe the principle to entail that we *do* have obligations under the PA scheme.

But it seems clear that Hart at least, and probably Rawls as well, did not mean for the principle to apply to such cases of "innocent bystanders." Hart, remember, begins his specification of the principle with: "When a number of persons conduct any joint enterprise. . . ." He then goes on to suggest that those who benefit from others following the rules are bound to cooperate as well. This way of stating the principle does seem to leave open the possible reading that anyone at all who benefits, whether he be a participant or not, is obligated to cooperate. And Nozick must be relying on such a reading if he believes his PA system case to be one to which Hart's principle applies. But this reading does not seem to capture the *spirit* of Hart's remarks; the beneficiaries who are bound under Hart's principle must, I think, be among those persons who are "conducting" the enterprise. This seems to me to be implicit in Hart's remarks. It is certainly a shame that he did not make it explicit, for that would have guarded the principle against the implausible sort of reading that Nozick utilizes, in which the principle binds *everyone* who benefits from the enterprise, regardless of his relation to it.

And a principle which had those results *would* be an outrageous one. People who have no significant relationship at all with some cooperative scheme may receive incidental benefits from its operation. Thus, imagine yourself a member of some scheme which benefits you immensely by increasing your income. Your friends and relatives may benefit incidentally from the scheme as well if, say, you now become prone to send them expensive presents. But the suggestion that their benefiting in this way obligates them to do their part in the scheme is absurd.

That Hart did not have in mind such an outrageous principle can be seen as follows, if any doubt remains. He wants the principle to serve in giving an account of political obligation. The benefits which citizens receive within the cooperative scheme of a political community may be thought of primarily as the benefits of the rule of law. It is the receipt of these benefits that binds each citizen to his fellow citizens. But, of course, other people besides citizens receive benefits from those citizens' maintaining the rule of law. People residing in neighboring nations, for instance, benefit from this. But Hart surely does not want to maintain that, e.g., Canadian citizens are bound to the political community in the United States simply because Canadians *also* benefit from the U.S. citizens' cooperative efforts to maintain the rule of law!

My suggestion is that Hart and Rawls should be read as holding that only beneficiaries who are also participants (in some significant sense) are bound under the principle of fair play. And on this reading, of course, Nozick's PA system example does not seem to be a case to which the principle applies; the individual in question is not a participant in the scheme, having had nothing to do with its institution, and having done nothing to lead anyone to believe that he wished to become involved in the scheme. The example, then, cannot serve as a counterexample to Hart's principle. In fact, all of Nozick's examples in his criticisms of Hart are examples in which an "outsider" has some benefit thrust on him by some cooperative scheme to which he is in no way tied (see Nozick's "street-sweeping," "lawn-mowing," and "book-thrusting" examples).[18] But if I am right, these examples do not tell against the principle of fair play, since the benefits accruing to "outsiders" are not thought by Hart and Rawls to bind under that principle.

The problem of specifying who are "outsiders," and consequently, whose benefits will count, is a serious one, especially in the political applications of the principle; I will have more to say about that in V.v. And it seems that the problem may provide ammunition for a serious counterattack by someone like Nozick against the principle of fair play. We have maintained, remember, that only "participants" or "insiders" in the cooperative scheme are candidates for being obligated under the principle to do their share in cooperating. Those "outsiders" who benefit from the scheme's operation are not bound under the principle of fair play. But how exactly do we differentiate between these outsiders and the insiders? What relationship must hold between an individual and a cooperative scheme for him to be said to be a participant in some significant sense?

This is a hard question to answer, but we have already considered some cases where an individual is *not* a participant in the right sense. Thus, merely being a member of some group, other members of which institute a scheme, is not enough to make one a participant or an "insider." Although Nozick's man is a "member" of an identifiable group, namely his neighborhood, this "membership" does not suffice to make him a participant in any scheme his neighbors dream up. Normally, we would want to say that for an individual to be a real participant in a cooperative scheme, he must have either 1) pledged his support, or tacitly agreed to be governed by the scheme's rules, or 2) played some active role in the scheme after its institution. It is not enough to be associated with the "schemers" in some vague way; one must go out and do things to become a participant or an "insider" and to potentially be bound under the principle of fair play.

Now, we can imagine an opponent of the principle accepting these remarks concerning whose benefiting will count, and accepting our criticism of Nozick's PA system counterexample, and still responding to our discussion by posing the following dilemma: We are agreed, the Nozickian begins, that "outsiders" fall outside the scope of Hart's principle; not just anyone who benefits from a cooperative scheme will be bound to do his share in it. And we are agreed that mere membership in some group, other members of which conduct some cooperative scheme, is insufficient to make one an "insider." And we are agreed that one becomes an "insider" by the means described above, perhaps among others. But the problem is this. In becoming an "insider," one must do something which involves either an express or a tacit undertaking to do one's part in the scheme. So if the principle of fair play can bind only "insiders" in a cooperative scheme, it will bind only those individuals who have *already* become bound to do their part in the scheme in becoming "insiders." The principle is superfluous; it collapses into a principle of consent. All and only those individuals who have actually undertaken to do their part in the scheme are bound by the principle of fair play to do their part in the scheme. Benefiting under the scheme is quite irrelevant, for benefiting only counts under the principle for "insiders." But "insiders" are already bound to the scheme, whether they benefit from it or not.

This argument, if it is acceptable, counts heavily against the principle of fair play, for that principle was supposed to show us how individuals could become bound to some cooperative enterprise *without* actually giving their consent to it. But if the principle can only plausibly be thought to bind those who have already consented to going along with the enterprise, the principle's usefulness becomes highly doubtful. We can explain whatever obligations participants in the enterprise are thought to have simply in terms of the principles of consent and fidelity, quite independent of considerations of fair play. We cannot become participants in the right sense without having given at least tacit consent to do our part in the scheme.

But is this sort of argument acceptable? Is it true that I cannot become a participant in the right sense without giving at least tacit consent to the scheme? Surely many participants in cooperative schemes have given their consent, either express or tacit, and are bound to their schemes regardless of what else they do to bind themselves. But these are not the individuals with whom Hart and Rawls are primarily concerned. With all our discussion of "participation," we are overlooking a feature of the principle of fair play which Rawls (and Hart, I've suggested) saw as essential to the generation of the obligation. The principle of fair play does not specify that all participants in cooperative schemes are bound to do their part, or even that all participants who benefit from the schemes are so bound. It states rather that those who *accept* the benefits of a cooperative scheme are bound to cooperate. This distinction between accepting benefits and merely receiving benefits has been lost somewhere in the shuffle. It is a distinction which is completely overlooked in Nozick's discussion of the principle of fair play. But it seems to me that this distinction is crucial in settling the problem of how to distinguish participants (or "insiders") from "outsiders."

For Rawls and Hart, the principle of fair play accounts for the obligations of those whose active role in the scheme consists of accepting the benefits of its workings. One becomes a participant in the scheme precisely by accepting the benefits it offers; the other ways in which one can become a participant are not important to considerations of fair play. And individuals who have merely *received* benefits from the scheme have the same status relative to it as those who have been unaffected by the scheme; they are not in any way bound to do their part in the scheme unless they have independently undertaken to do so. If, as I suggested, the acceptance of benefits constitutes the sort of "participation" in a scheme with which Rawls and Hart are concerned, we can understand why neither Rawls nor Hart specifically limits the application of the principle to *participants* in the scheme. This limitation has already been accomplished by making obligation conditional on the acceptance of benefits. This means, of course, that the principle cannot be read as the outrageous

one which requires anyone at all who benefits from the
scheme to do his part in it (this is the reading I earlier attributed to Nozick); it is limited in application to those
who are participants in the scheme, in the sense of having
accepted benefits.

But understanding the principle in this way also helps
us see why the Nozickian line of argument we have considered cannot succeed. The Nozickian tried to persuade
us that an individual could not become a participant, or
an "insider," without doing something which amounted
to giving his consent to do his part in the scheme. The obligations generated relative to the scheme could be explained in terms of consent. But it seems clear that a man
can accept benefits from a scheme, and be a participant in
that sense, without giving his consent to the scheme. And
further, such acceptance of benefits *does* seem to obligate
him to do his part. Let me support and clarify this claim
with an example.

Imagine that in Nozick's neighborhood the need for
public entertainment is not the only matter of concern.
There is also a problem with the neighborhood's water
supply; the water pumped through the pipes is sufficiently polluted to make nearly everyone desire corrective
action of some sort. But the government is sufficiently un-
responsive to make them sure that they will have to handle the problem themselves. So a neighborhood meeting
is called, at which a majority votes to dig a public well
near the center of the neighborhood, to be paid for and
maintained by the members of the neighborhood.

Some of the members clearly give their consent to the
proposed scheme. Others, who vote against the proposal,
do not. Jones, in particular, announces angrily that he
wants to have nothing to do with the scheme and that he
will certainly not pledge his support. Nothing, he claims,
could make him consent to such a ridiculous enterprise.
But in spite of his opposition, the well is dug, paid for,
and maintained by the other members of the neighbor-

hood. Jones, as expected, contributes nothing to this effort.

Now the benefits of clear, fresh water are available to the neighborhood, and Jones begins to be envious of his neighbors, who go to the well daily. So he goes to the well every night and, knowing that the water will never be missed, takes some home with him for the next day. It seems clear to me that Jones is a perfect example of a "free rider." And it also seems clear that, having accepted benefits from the scheme (indeed, he has gone out of his way to obtain them), he has an obligation to do his part within it. But he certainly does not seem to have *consented* to the scheme. We have, then, a case in which an individual has an obligation to do his part within a cooperative scheme which is *not* accounted for by a principle of consent. We would, I think, account for that obligation precisely in terms of fair play. Jones has made himself a participant in the scheme by accepting its benefits, although he has refused to give his consent.

So the Nozickian argument does not succeed. One might, rather feebly I think, try to maintain that Jones's taking the water was a way of giving tacit consent to the scheme. Hopefully, our discussion of consent in Chapter IV will have convinced the reader of the unpersuasiveness of such a position. But if not, we can suppose instead that Jones goes to the well during the day, taking the water while shouting, "Don't think this means I'm coming into your stupid scheme! I'll never consent to share the burdens of this enterprise!" Certainly under those conditions, to call the taking of the water a consensual act would be ludicrous.

I have tried to show, then, that the principle of fair play does not collapse into a principle of consent. While many participants in cooperative schemes will be bound to do their parts because they have consented to do so, many others will be bound because they have accepted benefits from the scheme. The obligations of the latter will fall under the principle of fair play. We should not think, because of the peculiarity of Jones's position in our example, that only the obligations of free riders like Jones will be accounted for by the principle. It is possible to go *along* with a cooperative scheme (as Jones does not) without consenting to it, becoming bound through one's acceptance of benefits. In fact, I think that *most* participants in cooperative schemes do nothing which can be thought to constitute consent. It is not necessary to refuse to give one's consent, as Jones does, in order not to give it. Consent is not given to a scheme by any behavior short of express dissent. Most participants in cooperative schemes simply "go along with" the schemes, taking their benefits and carrying their burdens. But if they do not expressly undertake to support the schemes, and if their behavior does not constitute a response to a clear choice situation, I do not think that we can ascribe consent to them. Certainly by going along with a scheme, we lead others to *expect* certain future performances from us; but this does not show that we have *undertaken* to perform according to expectations. Thus, the obligations which participants in cooperative schemes have (relative to those schemes) will not normally be grounded in consent. It remains to be seen, however, under what conditions any participants in a scheme can be obligated to do their parts in it, for we have not yet discussed carefully the important notion of the acceptance of benefits.

The reading of the principle which I have given obviously places a very heavy load on the notion of "acceptance," a notion to which we have as yet given no clear meaning. Rawls and Hart certainly give us no help on this count; in spite of the fact that Rawls stresses the need for "voluntary acceptance" in all of his accounts of the principle, he never gives us any clues as to what this "voluntary acceptance" is supposed to be. It is not, as I suggested in V.i, at all easy to distinguish in practice between benefits that have been accepted and those that have only been received, although some cases clearly seem to fall on the "merely received" side. Thus, benefits we have actively resisted getting, and those which we have gotten unknowingly or in ways over which we had no control at all, seem *not* to be benefits we have accepted. To have accepted a benefit, I think, we would want to say that an individual must either 1) have tried to get (and succeeded in getting) the benefit, or 2) have taken the benefit willingly and knowingly.

I suggested a moment ago that Nozick seems to have completely overlooked the distinction now under consideration. This can be seen in the fact that all of his supposed counterexamples to the principle seem to be cases of merely receiving, rather than accepting, benefits from some scheme (and this fact was, of course, responsible for my earlier charge that the individuals in Nozick's examples did not seem to be participants). But if the principle of fair play requires acceptance of benefits, then Nozick's examples may fail to be counterexamples.

Consider Nozick's examples of the programs that involve "thrusting books" into unsuspecting people's houses,[19] and the people on your street taking turns sweeping the street.[20] Clearly, the benefits in question are merely received, not accepted. "One cannot," Nozick writes, "whatever one's purposes, just act so as to give people benefits and then demand (or seize) payment. Nor can a group of persons do this."[21] I am suggesting, contra Nozick, that the principle of fair play does *not* involve justifying this sort of behavior; people are bound under the principle only when they have accepted benefits.

Nozick's first-line example, the PA scheme, however, is slightly more difficult. For here the benefits received are not forced upon you, as in the "book-thrusting" case, or gotten in some other way which is outside your control (as in the case of the person who mows your lawn while you're out of town, which I mentioned in V.i). Rather, the benefits are what I will call "open"; while they can be avoided, they cannot be avoided without considerable inconvenience. Thus, while I can avoid the (questionable) benefits the PA system provides by remaining indoors with the windows closed, this is a considerable inconvenience (and eventually, at least, more than this). The benefits are "open" in the sense that I cannot avoid receiving them, even if I want to, without altering my life-style (economists often have such benefits in mind in speaking of "public goods"). Many benefits yielded by cooperative schemes (in fact most benefits, I should think) are "open" in this way. A neighborhood organization's program to improve the neighborhood's appearance yields benefits which are "open." They cannot be avoided without avoiding the neighborhood altogether. And the benefits of government, which we have spoken of frequently, are mostly of this sort. The benefits of the rule of law, protection by the armed forces, pollution control, etc., can be avoided only by emigration.

We can contrast these cases of "open" benefits with benefits which are only "readily available." If instead of a PA system, Nozick's group had decided to rent a building in the middle of town in which live entertainment was continuously available to neighborhood members, the benefits of the scheme would only be "readily available." A good example of the distinction under consideration would be the distinction between two sorts of police protection, one sort being an "open" benefit, the other being only "readily available." Thus, the benefits which I receive from the continuous efforts of police officers who patrol the streets, capture criminals, and eliminate potential threats to my safety are benefits which are "open." They can be avoided only be leaving the area which the police force protects. But I may also request *special* protection by the police, if I fear for my life, say, or if I want my house to be watched while I'm away. These benefits are "readily available." Benefits which are "readily available" can be easily avoided without inconvenience.

Now, I think that clear cases of the acceptance of benefits, as opposed to receipt, will be easy to find where benefits which are only "readily available" are concerned.

Getting these benefits will involve going out of one's way, making some sort of effort to get the benefit, and hence there will generally be no question that the benefit was accepted in the sense we have described. It will be in cases like these that the principle of fair play seems most clearly to apply. These will be cases where our actions may clearly fall short of constituting *consent* to do our part in the scheme in question, but where our acceptance of benefits binds us to do our part because of considerations of fair play. When we accept benefits in such cases, it may be necessary that we be aware that the benefits in question *are* the fruits of a cooperative scheme, in order for us to be willing to ascribe any obligations of fair play; but it will *not* be necessary that some express or tacit act of consent have been performed.

The examples of "open" benefits are, of course, harder to handle. Nozick's comments seem quite reasonable with respect to them. Surely, it is very implausible to suggest that if we are unwilling to do our part, we must alter our life-styles in order to avoid enjoying these benefits. As Nozick suggests, there is certainly no reason why, when the street-sweeping scheme comes to your town, you must "imagine dirt as you traverse the street, so as not to benefit as a free rider."[22] Nozick's comments here do not, however, strike against the principle of fair play in any obvious way, for as I have interpreted it, the principle does not apply to cases of mere receipt of benefits from cooperative schemes; and the cases where the benefits are "open" in this way seem to be cases of mere receipt of benefits. Certainly, it would be peculiar if a man, who by simply going about his business in a normal fashion benefited unavoidably from some cooperative scheme, were told that he had voluntarily accepted benefits which generated for him a special obligation to do his part.

This problem of "acceptance" and "open benefits" is a serious one, and there are real difficulties involved in solving it. It may look, for instance, as if I am saying that a genuine acceptance of open benefits is impossible. But I would not want to be pushed so far. It seems to me that it is possible to accept a benefit which is (in one sense) unavoidable; but it is not at all the *normal* case that those who receive open benefits from a scheme have also accepted those benefits. In the case of benefits which are only "readily available," receipt of the benefits is generally *also* acceptance. But this is not so in the case of open benefits. I suggested earlier that accepting a benefit involved either (1) trying to get (and succeeding in getting) the benefit, or (2) taking the benefit willingly and knowingly. Getting benefits which are "readily available" normally involves (1), trying to get the benefit. It is not clear, however, how one would go about *trying* to get an open benefit which is not distributed by request but is rather received by everyone involved, whether they want it or not. If open benefits can be accepted, it would seem that method (2) of accepting benefits is the way in which this is normally accomplished. We can take the open benefits which we receive willingly and knowingly. But doing so involves a number of restrictions on our attitudes toward and beliefs about the open benefits we receive. We cannot, for instance, regard the benefits as having been forced upon us against our will, or think that the benefits are not worth the price we must pay for them. And taking the benefits "knowingly" seems to involve an understanding of the status of those benefits relative to the party providing them. Thus, in the case of open benefits provided by a cooperative scheme, we must understand that the benefits *are* provided by the cooperative scheme in order to accept them.

The necessity of satisfying such conditions, however, seems to significantly reduce the number of individuals who receive open benefits, who can be taken to have *accepted* those benefits. And it will by no means be a standard case in which all beneficiaries of a cooperative scheme's workings have accepted the benefits they receive.

I recognize, of course, that problems concerning "acceptance" remain. But even if they did not, my reading of the principle of fair play, as binding only those who have accepted benefits, would still face difficulties. The fact remains that we *do* criticize persons as "free riders" (i.e., in terms of fair play) for not doing their part, even when they have *not* accepted benefits from a cooperative scheme. We often criticize them merely because they *receive* benefits without doing their part in the cooperative scheme. Let us go back to Nozick's neighborhood and imagine another, more realistic, cooperative scheme in operation, this one designed to beautify the neighborhood by assigning to each resident a specific task involving landscaping or yard work. Homeowners are required to care for their yards and to do some work on community property on weekends. There are also a number of apartments in the neighborhood, but because the apartment grounds are cared for by the landlords, apartment dwellers are expected to help only on community property (they are expected to help because even tenants are granted full community membership and privileges; and it is reasoned that all residents have an equal interest in the neighborhood's appearance, at least during the time they remain there). Two of these apartment dwellers, Oscar and Willie, refuse to do their part in the scheme. Oscar refuses because he hates neatly trimmed yards, preferring crabgrass, long weeds, and scraggly bushes. The residents do not feel too badly about Oscar (although they try to force him out of the neighborhood), since he does not seem to be benefiting from their efforts without putting out. He hates what they are doing to the neighborhood. Willie, however, is another case altogether. He values a neat neighborhood as much as the others; but he values his spare time more than the others. While he enjoys a beautiful neighborhood, the part he is expected to play in the cooperative scheme involves too much of his time. He makes it clear that he would prefer to have an ugly neighborhood to joining such a scheme.

So while the others labor to produce an almost spotless

neighborhood, Willie enjoys the benefits resulting from their efforts while doing nothing to help. And it seems to me that Willie is *just* the sort of person who would be accused by the neighborhood council of "free riding," of unfairly benefiting from the cooperative efforts of others; for he receives exactly the same benefits as the others while contributing nothing. Yet Willie has not accepted the benefits in question, for he thinks that the price being demanded is too high. He would prefer doing without the benefits to having the benefits and the burdens.

So it looks as if the way in which we have filled out the principle of fair play is not entirely in accord with some common feelings about matters of fair play; for these common feelings do not seem to require acceptance of benefits within the scheme, as our version of the principle does. It is against these "ordinary feelings about fair play" (and not against the "filled-out" principle we have been describing), I think, that Nozick's arguments, and the "Nozickian" arguments we've suggested, strike most sharply.

But Willie's position is *not* substantially different from that of the salesman, Sam, whose sole territory is the neighborhood in question. Sam works eight hours every day in the neighborhood, enjoying its beauty, while Willie (away at work all day) may eke out his forty weekly hours of enjoyment if he stays home on weekends. Thus, Sam and Willie receive substantially the same benefits (if there is a "prestige" benefit which Willie receives from living in a beautiful neighborhood, we can imagine that Sam has a corresponding prestige in the fellowship of salesmen for having risen to being awarded such a beautiful territory). Neither Sam nor Willie has done anything at all to ally himself with the cooperative scheme, and neither has "accepted" the fruits of that scheme, although both "receive" them. Willie is a "member" of the community only because the council voted to award "membership" to tenants, and he has made no commitments; to make the parallel complete, we can even suppose that

Sam, beloved by all the residents, is named by the council an "honorary member." But if the neighborhood council accused Sam, the salesman, of "free riding," and demanded that *he* work on community property, their position would be laughable. Why, though, should Willie, who is like Sam in all important respects, be any *more* vulnerable to such accusations and demands?

The answer is that he is *not* any more vulnerable; if ordinary feelings about obligations of fair play insist that he *is* more vulnerable, those feelings are mistaken. But in fairness to Nozick, the way that Hart and Rawls phrase their account of the principle of fair play *does* sometimes look as if it expresses those (mistaken) feelings about fair play. As Rawls states it,

> The main idea is that when a number of persons engage in a mutually advantageous cooperative venture according to rules, and thus restrict their liberty in ways necessary to yield advantages for all, those who have submitted to these restrictions have a right to a similar acquiescence on the part of those who have benefited from their submission. We are not to gain from the cooperative labors of others without doing our fair share.[23]

This certainly looks like a condemnation of Willie's actions. Of course, the way in which Rawls fills out this idea, in terms of accepting benefits and taking advantage of the scheme, points in quite a different direction; for on the "filled-out" principle, Willie is not bound to cooperate, and neither is the salesman.

It looks, then, as if we have a choice to make between a very general principle (which binds all beneficiaries of a scheme) which is *very* implausible, and a more limited principle which is more plausible. I say that we have a choice to make simply because it seems clear that the limited principle is *much* more limited than either Hart or Rawls realized. For if my previous suggestions were correct, participants in cooperative schemes which produce "open" benefits will not always have a right to cooperation on the part of those who benefit from their labors. And this does not look like a result that either Hart or Rawls would be prepared to accept.

There is a great deal more that needs to be said about the principle of fair play, but this is not the place to say it. The results that we have produced to this point are adequate, I think, to evaluate the principle's usefulness in developing an account of political obligation. My arguments have suggested that the principle neither collapses altogether, as the "Nozickian" line of argument tried to persuade us, nor applies in as general a fashion as the Hart-Rawls account seems to want. What we must say about the political applications of the principle is, I assume, fairly obvious by now.

V.v. The Principle in Political Communities

When we move to political communities, the "schemes of social cooperation" with which we will be concerned will naturally be schemes on a rather grand scale. We may, with Rawls, think that the maintenance of the legal order should be "construed as a system of social cooperation,"[24] or perhaps we will want to identify all the workings of that set of political institutions governing "political society" generally as the operation of "the most complex example" of a cooperative scheme (as Hart seems to).[25] The details of the interpretation which we accept are not particularly important here. We must simply imagine a cooperative scheme large enough that "doing our part" will involve all of the things normally thought of as the requirements of political obligation; and regardless of how we characterize this scheme in its particulars, the difficulties which an account of political obligation utilizing the principle of fair play will involve, will be common to all particular versions. One limitation on this account, of course, is obvious from the start. Only political com-

munities which at least appear to be reasonably democratic will be candidates for a "fair play account" to begin
with. For only where we can see the political workings of
the society as a voluntary, cooperative venture will the
principle apply. Thus, a theorist who holds that the acceptance of benefits from a cooperative scheme is the *only*
ground of political obligation, will be forced to admit that
in at least a large number of nations, *no* citizens have
political obligations. Rawls recognizes this limitation,
claiming only that the principle accounts for political obligations in "constitutional democracies" (he, of course,
withdraws even this limited claim in *A Theory of Justice*).
Hart does not seem aware of the problem, but one assumes
that he would not disagree with Rawls's early position.

To return, whatever specific cooperative scheme we
identify as the one to be considered in giving an account
of political obligation using the principle of fair play, the
account will face problems that we have already discussed at length in the preceding portions of this chapter.
To begin, we face an immediate problem of "membership," of distinguishing the "insiders" from the "outsiders." Ideally, of course, the account wants all and only the
citizens of the state in question to be the "insiders" relative to the cooperative scheme in operation in the state.
The "all" in "all and only" can be sacrificed here, since an
account which only applies to some members of a political community is not obviously objectionable (II.ii); but
the "only" in "all and only" must not be compromised.
We cannot accept an account of political obligation which
binds noncitizens to do their part in a foreign country's
cooperative political enterprises.

But, as I suggested, the immediate problem lies in the
need to establish that at least a large number of citizens of
the states to which the principle is supposed to apply are
related to the scheme in the right way to be bound under
the principle. We are, after all, born into political communities; and being "dropped into" a cooperative scheme
does not seem significantly different from having a

scheme "built up around you," as in the cases mentioned earlier in V.iv. Most citizens, even in constitutional democracies, seem to be very much in the same sort of position as Nozick's man. They are not obviously tied to the grand cooperative scheme of political life any more than Nozick's man is tied to his PA scheme.

I tried to suggest earlier, of course, that the right way to distinguish the "insiders" relative to some scheme was through the notion of the "acceptance" of benefits from that scheme. While it is clear that at least most citizens in most states *receive* benefits from the workings of their legal and political institutions, how plausible is it to say that they have voluntarily *accepted* those benefits, in even the cases of the most democratic political societies now in existence? Not, I think, very plausible. The benefits in question have been mentioned before: the rule of law, protection by armed forces, pollution control, maintenance of highway systems, avenues of political participation, etc. But these benefits are what we have called "open" benefits. It is precisely in cases of such "open" benefits that it is least plausible to suggest that benefits are being *accepted* by most beneficiaries. It will, of course, be difficult to be certain about the acceptance of benefits in actual cases; but on any natural understanding of the notion of "acceptance" which seems relevant here, our having accepted open benefits involves our having had certain attitudes toward and beliefs about the benefits we have received (as noted in V.iv). Among other things, we must understand that the benefits flow from a cooperative scheme, rather than regarding them as "free" for the taking. And we must, for instance, think that the benefits we receive are worth the price we must pay for them, so that we would take the benefits if we had a choice between taking them (with the burdens involved) or leaving them. These kinds of beliefs and attitudes are necessary if the benefaction is to be plausibly regarded as constituting voluntary participation in the cooperative scheme.

But surely most of us do not have these requisite attitudes toward or beliefs about the benefits of government. At least many citizens barely notice (and seem disinclined to think about) the benefits they receive. And many more, faced with high taxes, with military service which may involve fighting in foreign "police actions," or with unreasonably restrictive laws governing private pleasures, believe that the benefits received from governments are not worth the price they are forced to pay. While such beliefs may be false, they seem nonetheless incompatible with the "acceptance" of the open benefits of government. Further, it must be admitted that, even in democratic political communities, these benefits are commonly regarded as purchased (with taxes) from a central authority, rather than as accepted from the cooperative efforts of our fellow citizens. We may feel, for instance, that if debts are owed at all, they are owed not to those around us, but to our government. Again, these attitudes seem inconsistent with the suggestion that the open benefits are accepted, in the strict sense of "acceptance." Most citizens will, I think, fall into one of these two classes: those who have not "accepted" because they have not taken the benefits (with accompanying burdens) willingly, and those who have not "accepted" because they do not regard the benefits of government as the products of a cooperative scheme. But if most citizens cannot be thought to have voluntarily accepted the benefits of government from the political cooperative scheme, then the fair play account of political obligation will not be suitably general in its application, even within democratic states. And if we try to make the account more general by removing the limitations set by our strict notion of "acceptance," we open the floodgates and turn the principle of fair play into the "outrageous" principle discussed earlier. We seem forced by such observations to conclude that citizens generally in no actual states will be bound under the principle of fair play.

These suggestions raise serious doubts about the Hart-Rawls contention that at least some organized political societies can be thought of as ongoing cooperative schemes on a very large scale. While such a claim may be initially attractive, does it really seem reasonable to think of any actual political communities on the model of the kinds of neighborhood cooperative schemes we have discussed in this chapter? This seems to me quite unrealistic. We must remember that where there is no consciousness of cooperation, no common plan or purpose, no cooperative scheme exists. I do not think that many of us can honestly say that we regard our political lives as a process of working together and making necessary sacrifices for the purpose of improving the common lot. The centrality and apparent independence of governments does not make it natural to think of political life in this way. No doubt we all have our own reasons for obeying the law and going along with the other demands made by our political systems. Prominent among these reasons, I suspect, are blind habit, fear of sanctions, and the conviction that some prohibited acts are "mala in se." Even among the thoughtful and "morally aware," it must be a rare individual who regards himself as engaged in an ongoing cooperative venture, obeying the law because fair play demands it, and with all of the citizens of his state as fellow participants.

Perhaps, then, we ought not to think of modern political communities as essentially or in part large-scale cooperative ventures. No doubt there is a sense in which society in general (and political society in particular) can be understood as a "cooperative venture," even though no consciousness of cooperation or common purpose is to be found. Social man is thought of as governed by public systems of rules designed to regulate his activities in ways which increase the benefits accruing to all. Perhaps it is this rather loose sense of "cooperative scheme" which Hart and Rawls have in mind when they imagine political communities as cooperative schemes.[8] But we should re-

---

[8] See Rawls, *A Theory of Justice*, e.g., pp. 4, 84. Rawls seems to be saying that a system of rules defines a cooperative scheme even where no individuals regard themselves as engaged in a cooperative scheme.

member that whatever intuitive plausibility the principle of fair play has derives from our regarding it as an acceptable moral principle for cooperative schemes in the *strict* sense. Clearly, the considerations which lead us to accept the principle of fair play as determining our obligations in the context of a neighborhood organization's cooperative programs may in no way be mirrored in the context of "cooperative schemes" understood in the loose sense mentioned above. So that while talk of cooperative schemes on the level of political communities may not be obviously objectionable, such cooperative schemes will not be among those to which we should be inclined to apply the principle of fair play.[26] All of this is not to say that we cannot *imagine* a political community being the sort of cooperative venture to the operations of which the principle of fair play might apply. In fact, we needn't imagine at all, since we have such a community painted in vivid detail in Rousseau's *Social Contract*. But Rousseau's society is not one with which we are familiar in actual political life.

These brief remarks all point toward the conclusion that at very best the principle of fair play can hope to account for the political obligations of only a very few citizens in a very few actual states; it is more likely, however, that it accounts for no such obligations at all. While we have seen that the principle does not "collapse" into a principle of consent, we have also seen that in an account of political obligation, the principle has very little to recommend it, either as a supplement to or a replacement for principles of fidelity and consent. In particular, the main advantage which the fair play account was thought to have over consent theory's account, namely, an advantage in *generality* (V.iii), turns out to be no advantage at all. We will not, then, advance very far with the suggestions of Hart and Rawls concerning the usefulness of the principle of fair play. And it seems that the principle will also not be able to help us solve the original problem with which this chapter began. It will not provide a satisfactory explanation of our intuitions concerning the binding character of Locke's "consent-implying enjoyments." With the failure of the principle of fair play, I will consider next a very different sort of approach to the problem, one which presents a "duty-centered" account of political obligation. This is the "mature" account given by John Rawls in *A Theory of Justice*, which centers on the "Natural Duty of Justice." It is to that account that I turn in Chapter VI.

CHAPTER VI

The Natural Duty
of Justice

VI.i. Rawls on Political Obligation

In *A Theory of Justice*, John Rawls is primarily concerned with principles for the evaluation of social and political institutions. But in Chapter VI he momentarily turns his attention to the moral principles for individuals, presenting interesting discussions of "the principle of fairness" and "the natural duty of justice." The result here is a different sort of answer to traditional difficulties over the problem of political obligation. Rawls's efforts on this topic merit examination; surprisingly, though, they have been one of the (relatively) ignored dimensions of an anything-but-ignored book. I will try to remedy that oversight. My remarks will center first, by way of introduction, on the manner in which the Rawlsian arguments can be seen to follow naturally from a consideration of the problem we have been discussing (the problem of finding a general ground for political obligation within the context of liberal political theory). Then I will turn to criticism, questioning from several angles the suitability of "the natural duty of justice" for the job Rawls intends it to do.

As I've suggested, I will be specifically concerned here, as Rawls obviously was, with the natural duty of justice only insofar as it is relevant to an account of our political bonds. But I shall try to treat Rawls's remarks on the subject independently of some aspects of the general argument in his book. In particular, I want to avoid emphasizing Rawls's argument that these moral requirements are the ones that would be chosen by his hypothetical original position contractors from a choice situation under conditions of partial ignorance. For, in the first place, I find Rawls's defense of this claim quite unconvincing;[f] more importantly, however, his arguments on these points stand on their own feet, independent of his unique "hypothetical contract" justifications.

Rawls's position in Chapter VI (and earlier, in sections 18 and 19) can be understood as a natural response to the problems encountered in trying to locate some plausible class of suitably voluntary acts on which to base a general political *obligation*. Thus, his transition to a "duty-centered" account of our political bonds can be seen as an answer to the following question: "In light of the failures

[f] Rawls gives us two reasons why he believes that the original position contractors would opt for his "duty-centered" account of our political bonds over the more traditional "obligation-centered" accounts. First, they would believe that basing our political bonds on obligations would "complicate the assurance problem" (p. 336). This is the problem of instability that arises when people have doubts about whether they and their fellow citizens are politically bound. If the performance of a voluntary act were required to become bound, such doubts could easily arise. Basing our political bonds on a duty (which requires no voluntary act to bind) is supposed to alleviate this problem, and so the original position contractors would opt for a duty-centered account. My remarks in VI.ii and VI.iii will suggest, however, that a similar "assurance problem" would arise concerning the citizens' justifiable doubts about whether the mere "application" of their political institutions is sufficient to bind them to compliance. The second reason Rawls gives for rejecting obligation-centered accounts is that the contractors would see that a voluntary act is not needed for "protection" against becoming bound to an unjust government (this "protection" was, of course, a major motivation for the development of consent theory's obligation-centered account—see III.ii). The natural duty specifies that institutions must be just for us to become bound to them, so that duty provides all the protection we need (pp. 335-336). But the "protection" provided by requiring a voluntary act (such as consent) for the generation of our political bonds, was not *just* protection against becoming bound to unjust regimes. It was protection against becoming bound to *any* government we find unsuitable, just or unjust (again, see III.ii). This aspect of the protection offered by the classical obligation-centered accounts is *not* preserved in the Rawlsian transition to a duty-centered account. That fact might very well influence the hypothetical choice Rawls describes.

of consent theory and the principle of fairness (or fair play) to provide a satisfactory account of our political bonds, what substance, if any, can we give to our belief that we are generally bound to support the political institutions of our country (at least when they are reasonably just)?" Rawls's answer is in part that the natural duty of justice successfully explains the moral basis for this firmly held belief. A great deal of argument, then, is presupposed (or only mentioned in passing) by Rawls. Specifically, it is only his belief that all obligation-centered accounts of our political bonds must fail (at least as *general* accounts) that allows him to assert that there is "no political obligation, strictly speaking, for citizens generally."[1]

We have, of course, already discussed the two most popular obligation-centered accounts, as well as the reasons for their failures. In Chapter IV we discussed the merits and shortcomings of consent theory and concluded that it could not provide a suitably general account of our political bonds. And in Chapter V we examined the account of political obligation which utilizes the principle of fair play, as this account was presented by Hart and Rawls. This account seemed to fail in part because of the difficulties involved in thinking of political communities as "cooperative schemes," and because citizens generally do not seem to have *accepted* the benefits of government. While Rawls, of course, was one of the prominent supporters of this fair play account of political obligation, in his more recent work he has rejected his earlier position.

Rawls first began to modify his "fair play account" of political obligation in his 1966 paper, "The Justification of Civil Disobedience,"[2] in which he presented a joint "fair play obligation-duty of justice" account of our political bonds. But it is not until *A Theory of Justice* that Rawls seems fully to realize the limitations of his principle of fair play, insofar as its political application is concerned. There the principle is renamed "the principle of fairness" and is modified slightly, but it remains substantially the same. But now, while he continues to accept that the principle may bind citizens who take special advantage of the benefits of government (e.g., by running for public office), Rawls denies that the principle of fairness binds citizens generally, even within just states. For under that principle, Rawls claims,

> Citizens would not be bound to even a just constitution unless they have accepted and intend to continue to accept its benefits. Moreover, this acceptance must be in some appropriate sense voluntary. But what is this sense? It is difficult to find a plausible account in the case of the political system into which we are born and begin our lives.[3]

Rawls appears here to have noted the difficulty in such political cases of drawing the distinction between merely receiving the benefits of government and voluntarily accepting those benefits. And he seems to conclude, as we did in V.v, that the suggestion that most citizens (even in just states) have accepted benefits is quite implausible. While Rawls is not explicit on these points, I take it that this difficulty with "acceptance" of benefits is at least most of what lies behind his change of heart concerning the principle of fair play.

But if there are (as Rawls assumes) no other obligation-centered accounts of our political bonds, beyond those offered by consent theory and the principle of fair play (the former is thought by Rawls merely to be a special application of the latter), then we must concede that citizens generally do not have political *obligations*. And when we have admitted this, only two options remain. Either we must accept the supposedly counterintuitive solution that most of us are not morally bound to support and comply with our political institutions, or we must try to find a duty-centered account of these bonds. Rawls, of course, selects the latter option.

VI.ii. When Institutions "Apply to Us"

The natural duty of justice binds each member of the political community to support and further the just political institutions of his country. It binds each member "irrespective of his voluntary acts, performative or otherwise,"[4] and is thus properly called a duty rather than an obligation. More specifically, the duty of justice has two parts: "First, we are to comply with and to do our share in just institutions when they exist and apply to us; and second, we are to assist in the establishment of just arrangements when they do not exist, at least when this can be done with little cost to ourselves."[5] This duty, then, provides us with a perfectly general account of political duty (for political communities governed by just institutions), in that all members of societies whose basic structures are just are bound equally under it (regardless of their individual performances or circumstances). Individuals living under unjust political institutions are not bound at all (for Rawls, even deliberate consent to an unjust institution's authority cannot bind one to it). Whatever scattered political *obligations* citizens may have merely "support" their political duty.

Now, I have no quarrel with the second clause of Rawls's duty of justice, which specifies that we are to assist to some extent in the establishment of just institutions. My difficulties are all with the first, and more central, requirement that we do our share in and comply with just institutions which apply to us. In particular, I want to raise some questions concerning the "application" of an institution to an individual.

What, after all, does it mean to say of a just institution that it "applies to us"? In order to know what we are bound to support and comply with under the duty of justice, of course, we must answer this question. Let us confine our attention to the case of political institutions, since that is our present concern. In that case, of course, it is easy enough to answer simply that the political and legal institutions of each country "apply to" people residing permanently within that country; and this seems probably to be what Rawls had in mind. But perhaps our answer here is too easy. For one still feels inclined to ask why, if this is all that "application" amounts to, the mere application of a just institution should be thought to bind us to comply with it.

Let me try to express my doubts by way of example. Imagine, to begin, that a group of benighted souls off in Montana organizes an "Institute for the Advancement of Philosophers," designed to help philosophers by disseminating papers, creating new job opportunities, offering special unemployment benefits, etc. Moreover, these benefits are distributed strictly according to the demands of justice; and they are made possible by the philosophers who pay "dues" to the Institute (such payment is the Institute's only requirement). One day the Institute, which has previously operated only in the West, decides to expand its operations eastward, and I receive in the mail a request that I pay my dues. Does this institution "apply to me"? There is a very weak sense in which we might say that it does; it is an institution for philosophers and I am a philosopher (of sorts). I may even stand to benefit from its operations in the future. But am I *duty-bound* to pay my dues, in accordance with the "rules" of the Institute? Perhaps we may say that I ought to do so, because such an institution is a good thing (but suppose that the dues are outrageously high?). I think it is clear, however, that I have no *duty* to "do my part" by paying dues. I am not morally required to go along with just any institution which "applies to" people of descriptions which I happen to meet, even if these institutions are *just*. People cannot simply force institutions on me, no matter how just, and force on me a moral bond to do my part in and comply with those institutions. Let us say that when an institution "applies to me" solely by virtue of my meeting a certain (morally neutral) description, the institution "applies to me weakly."

Now let us suppose that instead of having the institution "imposed" on me, I am born into the class of people to whom the institution "applies." Imagine that our Institute now plays a different role in the lives of philosophers, for, due to mounting social pressure, all philosophers have been forced to move into a small reservation in Gary, Indiana. The Institute begins to play a more active role. It fights to preserve the reputation of philosophers and lobbies in their interest; and while it still sends out letters telling philosophers to pay their dues, it now begins to enforce these demands, having formed a squad of hard-nosed Kantians to exact punishment for violations. It also begins to enforce other rules, rules against plagiarism, misrepresentation, committing modal fallacies, and discussing Merleau-Ponty. Gradually, the philosophers come to regard the Institute as having a right to enforce such rules (although at first there was resentment). And each child born on the reservation is now considered "a philosopher," at least until he expressly gives up the contemplative life and leaves the reservation.

What are we to say when I am born and grow up on the reservation? Does the institution in question "apply to me"? There is, I think, a fairly natural sense in which the answer is "yes." I am a "philosopher," and the Institute's rules are for philosophers. I follow the rules and am expected by others to do so. I even benefit from the Institute's workings, although these benefits I receive are all "open" benefits (V.iv), benefits in which all philosophers share whether they want to or not. But does it follow from this institution's "applying to me" in this sense that I am *morally required* to follow its rules if the institution is just? Does its applying to me in this way distinguish it in a morally significant way from other equally just institutions? I think not, for the thing which *makes* the institution apply to me here is the simple fact of my birth and growth in a territory within which the institution's rules are enforced; but my birth is not an act I perform, or something for which I am responsible. My suggestions here follow to a certain extent my remarks about "positional duties" in I.iii, where I argued that how I come to occupy a position makes all the difference in determining whether any moral requirements to perform my "positional duties" are generated. And my conclusion in I.iii does not seem to be altered by the mere fact that the institution which defines the position is *just*, regardless of our theory of justice. Let us say that when an institution "applies to me" as in the above example, it "applies to me territorially."

Finally, let us contrast the two cases outlined above with one in which I am an active participant in the activities of the institution, and am a member in the full sense of the word. I have given my express consent to be governed by its rules, or perhaps I have held office in the Institute or *accepted* (in the sense detailed in Chapter V) substantial benefits from the institution's workings. In such a case, the institution still seems to "apply to me territorially," but a new dimension is added. For now I have *done* things which seem to tie me to the Institute, rather than being a passive bystander. Let us say in this latter case that the institution "applies to me strongly."

Perhaps by now the point of these examples is becoming clear. The natural duty of justice is supposed to bind us only to those just institutions which "apply to us." We want to know why "application" should be significant in this way. What is it about a just institution's applying to me that makes it merit my special attentions? I have suggested that there is *nothing* morally significant about the "weak" or "territorial" senses of application, which hold when I simply am "specified" by the institution's rules or live in an area in which they are enforced. Only in cases of application in the "strong" sense, those that involve an individual's consent, say, or his *acceptance* of significant

benefits, does "application" begin to look morally important.

But if we return now to the political case, Rawls's natural duty of justice seems to face a serious problem. Rawls,
remember, wants this duty to bind all citizens to comply
with whatever just political institutions their countries
have to offer. But while the just political institutions of a
country certainly "apply to" that country's citizens, this is
always true only in the "territorial" sense of application.
And as a result, it does not appear that any duty to comply
would follow simply from that "application." What
would be needed, I have suggested, for such a duty to follow would be for the citizens to have performed certain
voluntary acts which make those institutions apply to
them in the "strong" sense. Thus, we are forced to read
"apply to us strongly" for "apply to us" in Rawls's statement of the duty of justice. But the acts which citizens
must perform in order to make their political institutions
apply in the "strong" sense are precisely those acts which
generate *obligations* under Rawls's principle of fair play
(and under the traditional principles of fidelity and consent which Rawls subsumes under that principle of fair
play). In that case, however, it looks as if the only citizens
who will be bound under this natural duty of justice will
be precisely those who have done things that have generated political *obligations* for them. And that means, of
course, that no more citizens will be bound under Rawls's
duty of justice than were already bound under traditional
principles of obligation.

Rawls's "perfectly general" account of our political
bonds, then, would seem in fact to be no more general
than the standard obligation-centered accounts. For it is
just as difficult to find people to whom political institutions apply in the "strong" sense as it is to find people
who are obligated to support those institutions (and the
weaker senses of application, to repeat, simply do not
allow us to derive the desired bond of compliance). The

significance of these results is that, first, Rawls has not succeeded in providing an account that applies more widely than do obligation-centered accounts, as he clearly intended to; only if we understand Rawls's "application clause" to concern "territorial" application does the natural duty of justice even appear to bind to compliance everyone living in a just state. But second, these considerations provide strong reasons for doubting that the "assurance problem" would favor Rawls's duty-centered account, and hence that the natural duty of justice would be chosen by Rawls's original position contractors (see note t).

We can put the point of my argument in another way by saying that Rawls's duty-centered account can accomplish its aims only by equivocating between two senses of "application." If we understand Rawls to be using the "territorial" sense of application in his formulation of the natural duty of justice, then just political institutions do indeed "apply to" all those residing within the state's domain. But in this case there is no reason to suppose (with Rawls) that any special duty to comply with or do our part in such institutions does follow from this "application." If, on the other hand, we take Rawls to be using the "strong" sense of application in his formulation of the duty, then all persons to whom the institutions apply *will* have a special duty (or, better, special obligations) to comply and do their part. But in this case, political institutions will *not* normally "apply to" all those who reside in the state. Rawls cannot have it both ways; either the natural duty he describes is not a genuine duty at all, or it is duty which seems to coincide with whatever obligations citizens already have toward their political institutions.

V.iii. Justice and Political Bonds

If my criticisms of the "application clause" of the natural duty of justice have been convincing, then a natural way to circumvent them would be to remove this clause from the specification of the duty. And this may seem to be a good idea for other reasons as well. For while it certainly seems true that the justice of an institution is a good reason to support it (so that it seems plausible to suggest that we have a duty to support just institutions), why should we believe that we are bound in any special way to support only those just institutions that "apply to us," as Rawls suggests? After all, the second part of the natural duty of justice requires us to assist in the establishment of just institutions *regardless* of their relation to us. And in an earlier version of the duty of justice (in "The Justification of Civil Disobedience"), Rawls did not attach the application clause to either part of the duty.[6] Why then does he include this troublesome clause in the latest version of the duty of justice?

One reason is undoubtedly a concern that without the application clause, the natural duty of justice seems to demand far "too much" of us. For without that clause the duty specifies that we are to comply with and do our share in just institutions *wherever* they are; and this, of course, is not just an unreasonable demand, but one that might be impossible to meet. It may seem, then, as if the application clause is absolutely essential to the coherent formulation of the duty of justice.

And in one respect this is true; if the duty of justice is to require compliance with and doing one's share in just institutions, then the application clause *is* necessary. But I want to ask why we should think that compliance with just institutions is a part of a duty of *justice*. Is it really the justice of the institution that is important here? I think not. The reason why the application clause appears to be necessary to the duty of justice is simply that an institution's applying to an individual in the "strong" sense *is*, as Rawls must have seen, a necessary condition of his being bound to comply with and do his part in it. But such "strong" application is also a *sufficient* condition for being so bound. This means that it is the "strong" application of the just institution that is important here, not the justice of that institution. That the institution in question is just is not the *ground* of the moral requirement in question. And this seems to show that by bringing the application clause into the natural duty of justice, we have surreptitiously imported an unrecognized ground of moral obligation into the duty.

It seems clear that the mere justice of an institution, which is the supposed ground of a duty to support just institutions, is insufficient to derive a moral requirement to comply with and do one's part in that institution. We are bound to comply and do our part only when the institution in question applies to us in the "strong" sense, that is to say, only when we have done certain things to make it apply to us. And those actions are themselves the grounds of obligations. By bringing this notion of application into a duty of justice, then, we turn the duty of justice into a special case (i.e., one limited to just institutions) of a duty "to fulfill obligations"!

But all of this is not to say that there is no natural duty of justice. I think that, as Rawls suggests, we do have a natural duty to support and assist in the formation of just institutions, at least so long as no great inconvenience to ourselves is involved. We do not, however, for the reasons I have suggested, have a natural duty to comply with or do our part in such institutions, whether or not they "apply to us." The duty of justice refers to just institutions wherever they may be and to whomever they apply. That a just institution "applies to us" seems quite irrelevant to the force of the moral argument at work here. Just institutions are the sort that ought to be promoted (for a variety of reasons), and it is this fact alone that is expressed by a duty of justice. No mention of "application" need be made. Of course, it is certainly true that just institutions which apply to us will normally be those which we will best be able to support, and in this sense "application" enters the picture. But here application is a matter of purely practical concern. Similarly, the duty to help those in need does not specify any privileged class of needers (e.g., those who are near at hand); the fact that an individual in need is nearby is merely a good practical reason for starting to do our duty in that case. In the same way, the fact that a just institution applies to us is only a good practical reason for supporting that particular just institution. But the application here has nothing to do with the ground of the duty. Rather, as I've suggested, the "strong application" of an institution to an individual has quite a different significance, insofar as it involves there having been some act performed which is itself the ground of a quite different sort of moral requirement. And the weaker applications of an institution to an individual have very little significance at all.

Of course, if we strip the natural duty of justice of its application clause in this way, and then are forced to strip it as well of its compliance clause, the resulting natural duty no longer looks like an appropriate tool for dealing with problems of political obligation. The natural duty of justice now becomes a duty merely to support and assist in the formation of just institutions; and this refers, of course, to all just institutions. But in that case, it is hard to see how such a duty could account for one being bound to one particular set of political institutions in any special way.

In order to see this point in its proper context, we must remember our initial discussion of the problem of political obligation in Chapter II; the "particularity requirement" is now a central concern. My conception of the problem of political obligation, remember, relates it closely to problems about citizenship; political obligation is something like the obligation to be a good citizen in a fairly minimal sense. As such, political obligation is the moral bond which ties an individual to one particular political community or set of political institutions in a special way. Now, a natural duty of justice binds me to support all just institutions, wherever they may be. It can bind me no more to one set of just political institutions than to any other. But this fails to capture the sense of political obligation sketched above. While, if my country's political structure is just, I am bound by the duty of justice to support it, there is nothing special about that bond. At the same time I am equally bound to support any other just political structure.

My suggestion, then, is that without some sort of application clause, the natural duty of justice will not help us answer questions about political obligation. But I have also given reasons for believing that the inclusion of such an application clause, as in Rawls's formulation, is illegitimate. If I am right in this, then, we must conclude that no headway on the problem of our political bonds will be made using a natural duty of justice. And, of course, it is easy to see that the points I have made lead also to the more general conclusion that no duty-centered account will fare any better. The reason is quite simple: the "personal transaction" feature of obligation-centered accounts is precisely what particularizes the moral requirement in the way necessary for an account of political obligation. And it is this feature that a duty-centered account, by definition, cannot share.

CHAPTER VII

Gratitude

VII.i. The Benefits of Government

In Chapters IV and V we discussed two prominent accounts of political obligation, the consent theory account and the account utilizing the principle of fair play. In both accounts the benefits provided by governments for their citizens were thought to be relevant to the existence of political obligations. While the two accounts differed concerning the significance of this benefaction, they agreed that the provision, receipt, or acceptance of the "benefits of government" was a necessary condition for the political obligations of at least many citizens.

In Chapter IV we saw how Locke (with many more recent consent theorists) attempted to add a special theory of "tacit consent" to the solid core of consent theory (which grounds political obligation in express acts of consent, promises, and contracts). For Locke the "giving" of tacit consent consisted precisely in the "enjoyment" of the benefits provided by the government. Thus, for Locke, the significance of the benefits of government to political obligation lay in the fact that their receipt by a citizen constituted consent (of a special sort) to the government's authority; the obligation grounded in this receipt of benefits was an "obligation of commitment." We showed in Chapter IV, however, that this account failed and that the receipt of the benefits of government could not be taken to constitute a citizen's "tacit consent."

In Chapter V we turned to the "fair play account" of political obligation; in that account the benefits of government played a different, but still central, role. The acceptance by a citizen of the benefits of government was construed as the acceptance of benefits accruing from the sacrifices of other participants in a cooperative scheme. Considerations of fair play were supposed to bind a citizen who accepts these benefits to do his share in the political community, and the obligation was then regarded as an "obligation of reciprocation." But, of course, we also rejected this "fair play account" of political obligation, along with its attempted explanation of the significance of the benefits of government to political obligation.

We have, then, to this point found no satisfactory explanation of the significance of these benefits; but neither have we found any reason to reject our original suggestion (II.ii) that the provision or receipt of the benefits of government seemed important to political obligation. Indeed, an account of political obligation which ignored the issue of benefits provided or received would undoubtedly fall subject to attack from a wide variety of positions, for we tend to feel strongly that, in the absence of an individual's consent to his government, the fact that he does not benefit from the rule of his government establishes that he cannot be bound to support or obey it; those who do not receive significant benefits from the workings of their legal and political institutions seem to owe no allegiance to the governments of their countries of residence (provided only that they have not consented, promised, or contracted in such a way as to generate this bond). And if that is true, then the receipt of the benefits of government must be either a ground of or a necessary condition for any political obligation which is not grounded in consent.

This view is widespread even among those writers who have no specific account of why these benefits are important to political obligation. Jeffrie Murphy puts the point this way: "I am inclined to think that those people who are systematically excluded from the benefits of a society do not have any moral obligation to obey that society's laws as such."[1] Murphy has in mind here the position of oppressed minorities, who are denied (at least some of) the significant benefits of government. And A. C. Ewing makes the same sort of claim; because the benefits of government have not been conferred upon them, Ewing writes, "at least certain large classes of poverty-stricken slum dwellers have no special obligation to their country."[2] It should be noted that oppressed minorities are not (at least normally) denied *all* of the benefits of government, as Murphy and Ewing seem to suggest; so that insofar as political obligations are thought to be grounded merely in the receipt of the benefits of government (as opposed to, say, the receipt of a certain "reasonable share" of these benefits), the conclusion that the oppressed owe no obligation seems unjustified. A more natural conclusion, given that assumption, would be that the oppressed owe less to the government than their more fortunate fellow citizens.[3]

An easier test of the view that we are examining would be a case in which a citizen actually received none of the benefits of government. Such a case is not difficult to construct. Imagine a fur trapper whose home lies in some desolate province of an otherwise civilized and politically organized nation. Because of limited resources available to the government, the government is never able to extend any of the benefits it provides for its other citizens to this isolated corner of its domain. Police forces do not operate there, the armed forces do not protect it from invasion, and in general the government leaves the area completely on its own. Can we seriously maintain that the trapper is bound to support and comply with the government of the state, simply because he lives within the recognized boundaries of the state?[u] Is he bound to comply with the country's gun control laws, or to fight in the armed forces when the call goes out for able-bodied men? Surely not. If

[u] It may, of course, seem that even isolated as he is, the trapper must be receiving *some* benefits. If he were found to be injured, or starving, or if he were threatened by others, the government would intervene in his interest; it would provide for him if it knew that aid was needed. But I am not confident that this is a significant benefit where there is little chance that the government will ever obtain such knowledge, and where it makes no real effort to obtain it. It seems fair to say that any "benefits" we imagine will be too slight to affect our argument.

my example seems too fanciful, think of the "mountain men" of early America, or the nomads of eastern Russia. Or imagine the position of the natives of Guam who, after Balboa claimed the Pacific, became subjects of the Spanish Empire in the eyes of the world. Would anyone claim that they owed new obligations to a government which did not even know of their existence?

Our confidence that such individuals are not bound to the governments in whose domains they reside is based, I think, primarily in our recognition that they have not shared in the benefits those governments provide to other citizens. And this suggests that the receipt or provision of the benefits of government, if improperly explained in terms of consent or fair play, is nonetheless relevant to political obligation. In this chapter I will consider a third account of this relevance. The position to be examined holds that political obligations are generated by the receipt of the benefits of government under a principle of *gratitude* (the second moral principle accounting for "obligations of reciprocation"), which requires that we repay our benefactors. Because of considerations of gratitude, we are bound to a government which bestows upon us significant benefits. These claims need considerable filling out, of course, but the important thing to note at this point is the moral principle which has been brought into play, the principle of gratitude.

This sort of position is first defended by Socrates in Plato's *Crito*. In the words of "the Laws":

> Are you not grateful to those of us laws which were instituted for this end, for requiring your father to give you a cultural and physical education? . . . Then since you have been born and brought up and educated, can you deny . . . that you were our child and servant, both you and your ancestors? . . . We have brought you into the world and reared you and educated you, and given you and all your fellow citizens a share in all the good things at our disposal.[4]

It is, of course, a bit difficult to see how "the Laws" can be taken to have "brought you into the world," or, indeed, to have done most of the things which Socrates attributes to them. But there is no denying that most of us do receive substantial benefits from the workings of our legal institutions, and from governments generally, even if the benefits we receive are not the ones which Socrates names. So we can take Socrates to be arguing simply that we owe a "debt of gratitude" to our government for the benefits with which it has provided us, just as we owe such a debt to our parents. Socrates relies in his argument on this comparison between political and "filial" obligations, and this Socratic lead is followed in many more recent discussions of political obligation. Ewing, for instance, observes:

> The obligation to one's country or state is more analogous to the obligation to our parents than it is to a business relation. Here also the debt is not incurred deliberately . . . and here also it seems to depend, mainly at least, on uncovenanted benefits conferred on us.[5]

It should be stated that two highly questionable premises are employed in the "Socratic argument." First, it is assumed that we do owe debts of gratitude to our parents for the care they have given us. Not only Socrates, but nearly every philosopher since who has written on the subject of gratitude has made this same assumption; I will present some considerations in VII.ii, however, which militate against this choice for a paradigm of debts of gratitude. Second, the Socratic argument assumes that the analogy between the parent-child and state-citizen relationships is complete enough to support the claim that if children are obligated to their parents, then citizens are bound to their states. But for this assumption to be justified, more points of similarity will be required to bolster the alleged analogy than the mere fact that benefits are provided in both cases. For no one believes that the mere provision of benefits to a person, *regardless* of the conditions under which this is accomplished, will be sufficient to generate an obligation.

For the Socratic argument (which relies for much of its force on our feelings of indebtedness to our parents) to succeed, then, it must show two things. First, it must show that we do in fact owe debts of gratitude to our parents; and second, it must show that there are no morally relevant points of dissimilarity between the parent-child and state-citizen relationships, which would defeat the move from "filial" to political obligations. But this second task, at least, clearly seems to be impossible to perform. At least since Locke's *Two Treatises* it has been widely accepted that the purported analogy between the political and familial relationships is something less than compelling. Indeed, it takes very little imagination to see the manifold points of dissimilarity (beginning, most importantly, with the unquestionable responsibility which a parent has to his child, and the fact that a child is neither fully rational nor sufficiently experienced to live without guidance and care; neither feature is obviously mirrored in the case of the state and the citizen; there are, of course, other clear points of dissimilarity).

In order to advance an account of political obligation which utilizes a principle of gratitude, it is not, however, necessary to rely in this way on a comparison with debts owed to our parents. And in fact, because of doubts we may justifiably have concerning the existence of such "filial" debts, the "gratitude account" becomes both simpler and more plausible in the absence of a such a reliance. W. D. Ross and J. P. Plamenatz both briefly defend the gratitude account without relying on any comparisons between the parent-child and state-citizen relationships. Ross writes: "The duty of obeying the laws of one's country arises partly . . . from the duty of gratitude for the benefits one has received from it. . . ."[6] And Plamenatz states:

Nor does it follow, because to live under the protection of a certain government and under the protection of certain laws does not constitute consent to the existence of that government and those laws, that it does not impose upon the protected person an obligation to obey them. The obligation, in this instance, would not arise out of consent, but would be no more than a special case of the general obligation to help persons who benefit us.[7]

Neither Ross nor Plamenatz commits himself to the "child-parent" model as a paradigm of debts of gratitude; but perhaps this is only because they do not commit themselves to any model as a paradigm. As it stands, the "gratitude account" that we have mentioned, and that Ross and Plamenatz support, is no more than a skeleton of an account. It cannot be evaluated until we have a general understanding of "debts of gratitude," which will allow us to determine whether the provision or receipt of the benefits of government meets the conditions necessary for the generation of such debts. Section VII.ii will be directed toward achieving that general understanding.

VII.ii. Debts of Gratitude

Gratitude has not been discussed very often in recent moral philosophy; Ross was probably the last major moral philosopher to seriously consider gratitude as a source of moral requirements.[8] (There are, of course, a few exceptions to this general contemporary neglect of gratitude.)[9] And there are, I think, good reasons which explain the paucity of philosophical literature on the subject. First, of course, is the widespread uncertainty about the existence of "debts" or "obligations" of gratitude, when compared with, say, obligations to keep promises. Second, it is very difficult to see whether considerations of gratitude fall properly within the realm of morality at all; the triviality of most "debts of gratitude" (which involve no more than saying "thank you" or writing a note of thanks) seems to place them more properly in the realm of etiquette. And the very ritualized performances involved would support this conclusion. In one recent paper on gratitude, Daniel Lyons speaks of rules concerning gratitude as "norms of etiquette";[10] his discussion makes it clear that he does not regard "debts of gratitude" as serious moral requirements.

And yet it seems clear to me that in at least some cases considerations of gratitude will require performances which are neither trivial nor highly ritualized and which go beyond mere expressions of thankfulness. Typically, obligations of gratitude in such cases will involve making up for sacrifices made or losses incurred by another in the act of rendering us assistance or providing us with bene-fits. Much more, of course, needs to be said about these suggestions. But it is worth noting here that philosophers in previous centuries, if not in this one, have been not at all uncomfortable with the suggestion that considerations of gratitude may require nontrivial performances; in fact, obligations of gratitude were treated as very important in moral philosophy prior to the twentieth century, and the failure to fulfill such obligations was regarded as a serious moral shortcoming. Thus Hume, for instance, wrote: "Of all the crimes that human creatures are capable, the most horrid and unnatural is ingratitude, especially when it is committed against parents. . . ."[11] And for Kant, ingrati-tude was one of the vices which are "the essence of vileness and wickedness."[12] These passages echo the sen-timents of Shakespeare's King Lear, horrified at his daughter's failure to discharge what are constantly called "her obligations": "How sharper than a serpent's tooth it is to have a thankless child. . . . Ingratitude, thou marble-hearted fiend, more hideous when thou show'st thee in a child than the sea-monster!" (King Lear, I, iv.)

Once again in these passages, as in Socrates's argument, the supposedly paradigmatic obligation of gratitude which children are thought to owe to their parents comes to the fore. And it may appear that those who have thought debts of gratitude to be important were primarily parents, outraged at the "undutiful" behavior of their children, or fearing such behavior. Certainly the "gratitude" which parents think themselves owed by their children often consists in wholly unreasonable restraints on the actions of their children. But most of the philosophers who regarded gratitude as important were not motivated by such questionable concerns. They took debts of gratitude seriously for a number of reasons, of which perhaps the most important was that considerations of gratitude were supposed to account for our obligations to God. But many of these philosophers also believed that obligations of gratitude were important because of the central role gratitude seemed to them to play in promoting mutual trust and benevolence among men. Hobbes, for instance, had gratitude required by a "Law of Nature" (the fourth) because of the great importance of not discouraging benevolent action.[13] This lead is followed later by Price and Kant. Richard Price makes "Gratitude" one of his six "heads of duty," noting that "the consideration that we have received benefits, lays us under peculiar obligations to the persons who have conferred them"; he justifies his claim by reference to the "utility" of a duty of gratitude.[14] And for Kant, gratitude "must be regarded especially as a sacred duty . . . whose violation . . . can destroy the moral incentive for benevolence."[15]

Moreover, obligations of gratitude, which are today looked upon with some suspicion, were taken prior to this century to be particularly clear sorts of obligations, much as obligations to keep promises have always been thought to be. Thus, Sidgwick noted that "where gratitude is due, the obligation is especially clear and simple. Indeed the duty of requiting benefits seems to be recognized wherever morality extends."[16] And earlier (1734) John Balguy wrote: "That a man ought to be grateful to his benefactors, may be looked upon as equivalent to a self-evident proposition."[17] In another passage Balguy makes what we would today call an "argument from ordinary language" in support of this claim of "self-evidence": "The ideas of benefits and obligations are so closely connected, that to 'do a man a kindness' and to 'oblige him,' are used promiscuously, as expressions of the same significance."[18]

No one today would try to defend Balguy's claim that his proposition is "self-evident"; nor can we share the belief (expressed in several of the passages above) that just *any* provision of benefits generates obligations of gratitude. But I do want to press my claim that there are genuine obligations of gratitude, even if I must reject the largely uncritical enthusiasm about such obligations which is in evidence in many of the passages from earlier philosophers cited above. Let me begin to try to be more precise about those points that I think these philosophers have overlooked.

To begin, we can ask what exactly would be owed if one did have an obligation of gratitude, for there is an initial unclarity on this point (that remains uncorrected in most of the accounts mentioned above). The "crime" of ingratitude seems to refer to deficiencies in either or both of two areas. One can be "ungrateful" if one fails to *feel* certain things (i.e., feelings of gratitude), or one can be "ungrateful" if one fails in certain *outward* performances (even if I feel grateful, my failure to express this gratitude somehow through action may earn me a charge of "ingratitude"). When I am under an obligation of gratitude, then, am I bound to feel something, to complete some outward performance, or both? Sidgwick, in the passage cited above, equates the duty of gratitude with that of "requiting benefits," and seems to go on to allow that a mere outward performance is all that is required by the duty. Kant, characteristically, recognizes duties to both "active" and "affective" gratitude.[19]

But surely we would have a great deal of difficulty in making sense of a duty or obligation to feel a certain way. Moral requirements are generally supposed to range over our *actions*; having certain feelings (or experiencing certain emotions) seems inappropriate as the content of a moral requirement. The reason for this is, I think, quite simple. We are presumed to have a kind of control over our actions that we do not have over our feelings; we can, at least normally, *try* to act in specified ways, where we cannot try to have certain emotions or feelings (in the same way). And surely part of the point of a moral requirement is that its content be the sort of thing which we can, at least normally, *try* to accomplish. More, of course, needs to be said about the line of argument I am suggesting here. But it would not pay us, I think, to pursue the topic at length. For even if part of the content of an obligation of gratitude were having a certain feeling, this would not help us to get any clearer about the problem of *political* obligation. For political obligation is an obligation to *act* in certain ways. I think it is clear that debts of gratitude bind us at least to the performance of certain acts, and beyond this fact no other discoveries would be relevant to a political obligation accounted for by the principle of gratitude. I will assume, for simplicity's sake, that nothing more than acts are required under the principle of gratitude (and in this I follow Sidgwick, as mentioned previously, as well as Ross);[20] but this assumption will beg no questions about political obligation.

"Feelings of gratitude" aside, it is not easy to say even what acts are required by "obligations of gratitude."[v] Even in particular cases, this often seems quite unclear. Unlike the obligation to honor a promise or a contract, where the content of the obligation is usually determined with some precision by the terms of the agreement, obligations of

[v] My decision to call them *obligations* of gratitude rather than *duties* of gratitude is a fairly arbitrary one. The moral bond in question has interesting features which make it look both like a duty and like an obligation. No voluntary act is required for its generation, a feature characteristic of (in fact, on the view I defended in Chapter I, *definitive* of) duties. On the other hand, the bond has the nature of a "debt" and involves a personal transaction (i.e., past services rendered), which features are

gratitude are more often less "content-specific." What we think that an obligation of gratitude requires an individual to do will turn, of course, on the needs of the original benefactor and the position of the original beneficiary; but even when these factors are weighed, it will often be difficult to say that this or that particular act is required, or that some performance has discharged the obligation. Most often in acknowledging an obligation of gratitude to another, we are acknowledging a very general sort of indebtedness and an obligation to consider the interests of the obligee (the one to whom the obligation is owed) in a special way in the future. When a man says (seriously, and meaning it literally) "I am greatly indebted to you," he may be recognizing such an obligation of gratitude, even if he can tell us nothing at all about what he believes himself to be obligated to do (beyond the general sort of notion of indebtedness mentioned above).

I will have more to say about the content of obligations of gratitude momentarily. I suspect that this "vagueness" in content has a great deal to do with the suspicions we may have about the existence of such obligations; but given the confusing vagueness of other sorts of duties, and the uncertainty most of us feel about the pursuit of moral ideals in general, it seems unfair to "dismiss" obligations of gratitude on account of the vagueness of their content. At any rate, even if all that I have suggested to this point has been accepted, we have not yet advanced very far in our understanding of obligations of gratitude; we have established only that an obligation of gratitude requires some conduct which will serve as the requital of benefits granted by another. But clearly there are many instances in which benefits are granted where we would be

---

characteristic of obligations. If we choose to call the bond a "duty," we must keep in mind that it is a duty activated by a personal rendering of services. I have chosen to call debts of gratitude "obligations" primarily to emphasize the fact that they will be *particularized* in the way we want for an account of political obligation—the same moral bond will not bind us to different political communities under a principle of gratitude.

unwilling to allow that any obligation was generated thereby for the recipient of those benefits. In Chapter V, for instance, we noted in our "mad doctor" example that benefits *forced* upon us against our will could not be taken to give rise to any obligation of repayment (this point will be discussed further in condition 3 below). And there will be other cases where the simple receipt of benefits will not be sufficient for the generation of an obligation. What I want to do now is to suggest what seem to me to be the most obvious sorts of conditions which must be met if the receipt of benefits is to generate an obligation of gratitude; I present them only as necessary conditions, which may not be jointly sufficient.

Two variables suggest themselves immediately as being relevant to whether anything, and if so what, is owed because of considerations of gratitude. Sidgwick labels them "the effort made by the benefactor" and "the service rendered to the benefited"[21] (Berger[22] and Kant[23] also pick these variables). Taking the latter first, it is clear that the value of the benefit to the beneficiary will in some way be relevant to at least the *content* of a debt of gratitude, if not to its generation. It might even seem that, other things being equal, the "size" of the debt would vary directly with the value of the benefit received. But this would be mistaken. No one would maintain that the difference between what I owe a man who saves my life and what I owe a man who saves, say, my house is equivalent to the difference in value to me of my life and my house. And clearly, in neither case do I owe the man an amount equivalent to, say, the cash value I would place on my life or my house; so the suggestion of *equal* return being required seems implausible as well.[24] In general, the limits which the value of the benefit received places on the debt generated seem to be very vague indeed. We can usually specify some forms of repayment which would be inappropriate, and the value of the benefit will be important in this; and if the value of the benefit is small enough, it may even be that no such obligation is generated. But it will normally be difficult to specify any relation which should hold between the value of the benefit and the value of the repayment (and even if we could specify such a relation, the problems of weighting and ranking "values" would be insuperable). Similarly, it will be difficult to balance the value of the benefit received against other variables, such as the effort made by the benefactor, in any precise way. To quote Sidgwick once more:

> If a poor man sees a rich one drowning and pulls him out of the water, we do not think that the latter is bound to give as a reward what he would have been willing to give for his life. Still, we should think him niggardly if he only gave his preserver half-a-crown; which might, however be profuse repayment for the cost of the exertion. Something between the two seems to suit our moral taste: but I find no clear accepted principle upon which the amount can be decided.[25]

Let us return now to a statement of the conditions necessary for the receipt of benefits to generate an obligation of gratitude. The first two conditions will concern the benefactor's role in the process.

1. First, of course, we can consider the role of "the effort made by the benefactor," which was mentioned a moment ago. It seems quite clear that where an obligation of gratitude is owed to the benefactor, he must have made some special effort or sacrifice, or incurred some loss, in providing the benefit in question. If a person benefits us by merely pursuing his own business, we do not feel any special debt is owed him. If, for instance, I am being mugged in an alley when a man's walking past frightens my assailant away, I will not owe that man any special debt of gratitude. His appearance was only a happy coincidence, which cost him nothing. I may be *grateful* that he happened by, but we must distinguish this carefully from my owing him a debt of gratitude. I may also be grateful that my cab's being late forced me to miss my plane, a

plane which subsequently crashed. But certainly I have no obligation to either the cab or its driver. The idea here is that what is owed in a debt of gratitude is something which is thought to repay, or make up for, the effort or loss of the benefactor.

And this, of course, suggests a further specification of the content of obligations of gratitude. In many cases, some of the requirements of gratitude will be obvious in light of the losses incurred by the benefactor in providing us with some benefit. If a man burns his arms in pulling me from a flaming wreck, I will owe him, if nothing else, the medical treatment his burns require. If I break an axle on my car in rushing a dying man to a hospital over rough terrain, I may expect him to pay for repairing my car. These seem to me to be the clearest sorts of examples of repayments due because of considerations of gratitude; but they are also examples not of repaying a special effort, but rather of a direct "reimbursement" for losses incurred *in the process of* making that special effort. These sorts of debts of gratitude are in a sense preliminary. For we think that gratitude *also* requires some sort of repayment for the effort itself, and for things like pain and risk and time spent, for which there is no easy method of compensation. Here again, even in particular cases, the content of the debt will be very vague.

2. In addition to our first requirement of a special effort or sacrifice, however, there are other features of the benefactor's performance necessary to the generation of an obligation of gratitude. These features concern the benefactor's *reasons* for granting the benefit. First, his provision of the benefit must be intentional if we are to owe him a debt of gratitude for his performance;[26] a benefit which he gives us unintentionally will not bind us to any repayment. Second, he must have given the benefit voluntarily. A man who benefits me because of the gun at his back does not earn my gratitude, although he may, for instance, be entitled to ask for a return of the benefit (if possible) when the gunman no longer is in control. Third, the

benefactor must not have provided the benefit for reasons of self-interest. The politician who distributes favors only because he hopes to receive votes in return, and the industrialist who builds new homes for the poor only because their old homes stood on a desirable site for his new factory are not owed a debt of gratitude by those they have benefited. While again we may be "grateful that" the benefits were provided for us, the benefactor is owed no debt of gratitude if those benefits were provided for the wrong reasons. For the phrase "grateful that" in the preceding sentence really means nothing more than "pleased that"; the "gratefulness" involved is directed only at a state of affairs, rather than at a benefactor. When a man benefits us in order to advance his own interests, he will not earn our gratitude, for he treats us simply as a means to an end. As P. F. Strawson puts it:

> If someone's actions help me to some benefit I desire, then I am benefitted in any case; but if he intended them so to benefit me because of his general goodwill towards me, I shall reasonably feel a gratitude which I should not feel at all if the benefit was an incidental consequence, unintended or even regretted by him, of some plan of action with a different aim.[27]

This discussion will help us to see the contrast between a principle of gratitude and the other sort of "principle of reciprocation" which we have discussed, the principle of fair play. Under the principle of fair play, an individual's sacrifices within a cooperative scheme may create for others an obligation to repay him, even if the individual's *reasons* for making the sacrifices were purely self-interested (i.e., the sacrifices were made *only* for the sake of the benefits which will accrue to him from the reciprocal sacrifices of others). In fact, the whole idea behind the sorts of cooperative schemes Hart and Rawls have in mind is that the participants are not acting in order to benefit others, but rather in order to benefit everyone, themselves importantly included. Thus, a man acting selfishly could fit into a cooperative scheme and be one of those to whom others owed "obligations of reciprocation"; his reasons for cooperating are not important. But a man who provided benefits to another for purely selfish reasons could *not* be owed an obligation of gratitude; here his reasons for providing the benefits are a crucial consideration. Thus, if any obligation is to be generated by the provision of benefits to others for *selfish* reasons, the context of a *cooperative scheme* within which these benefits are provided (here assuming that by cooperating I benefit others in the scheme) is absolutely necessary.

And part of what made Nozick's criticism of "Hart's principle" so misleading, was precisely Nozick's failure to see the crucial role which the "cooperative context" plays in the principle of fair play. We have, of course, already discussed Nozick's attack on the principle of fair play in Chapter V; but it is only in the context of our present discussion of gratitude that one of the real problems with that attack can be stated clearly. For while Nozick takes himself to be challenging the principle of fair play, the principle against which Nozick's examples really tell is not the principle of fair play at all, but rather some sort of very loose "gratitude to a group" principle. Nozick's examples are of two types in which either individuals or groups force benefits on "innocent bystanders." Significantly, he shows us that he must regard the *group* principle that he is attacking as a mere extension of some *individual* principle, when he says: "One cannot, whatever one's purposes, just act so as to give people benefits and then demand (or seize) payment. Nor can a group of persons do this."[28]

Now, the individual principle Nozick is rejecting must be something like a principle of gratitude (but one lacking the restrictions I am recommending). And he is *right*, of course, that, e.g., when a person comes and thrusts books into my home[29] I am not obligated to repay him, for obvious reasons; the benefits are forced on me, may not be wanted by me, and are provided for the wrong reasons (i.e., they are provided as a necessary side effect of an activity being pursued for the satisfaction of the "book-thruster"). All of these facts establish that no obligation of gratitude is generated in Nozick's "individual cases." But from the passage cited above, and from the structure of his "group cases," the "group principle" that Nozick is attacking appears to be something like a principle of "gratitude to a group" (again, without the proper restrictions incorporated), which directs us to repay benefits provided for us by a group of individuals. And, of course, Nozick is *again* correct in denying that the individuals in his examples are bound under this "group principle," for the simple reason that the principle is not valid; the same sorts of constraints that apply to the individual principle are required here.

But this loose "gratitude to a group" principle which Nozick's examples successfully attack is *not* the principle of fair play. Hart and Rawls did not conceive of the principle of fair play as a simple "group version" of a principle of gratitude (and they certainly would not have supported the "gratitude to a group" principle I have described, a principle incorporating none of the obviously necessary restrictions). The obligations generated under the principle of fair play turn crucially on the individual's role as a participant in a *cooperative scheme*; it is not enough, as in Nozick's examples, that I simply receive benefits from a group of people. Free riding within a cooperative scheme is not supposed to be a simple case of treating others badly by not being grateful for the benefits they have granted. Free riding treats others badly by taking advantage of sacrifices they make in good faith, and by endangering the whole beneficial structure. Thus, the principle of fair play is not the principle against which Nozick's examples tell; his examples are successful only in pointing out the defects of a "gratitude to a group" principle (which lacks the necessary restrictions). Nozick would not, of course, be happy with this description of his arguments; he certainly did not intend to be attacking this "gratitude to a group" principle. But given his neglect throughout of the requirement that an individual be an active participant in a cooperative scheme (as opposed to a nonparticipant being benefited by a group) in order to be bound under the principle, I do not think this account of the actual force of Nozick's argument is unfair.

Let us return now to our discussion of condition 2 for the generation of obligations of gratitude. We have noted thus far that no debt of gratitude is owed to an individual who provides us with benefits unintentionally, involuntarily, or for reasons of self-interest. But we should observe here that self-interest is not the *only* motive which is unacceptable in this way.[30] If, for instance, my benefactor has provided me with benefits because it will hurt someone else (i.e., out of malice), no debt of gratitude is generated; when the dying man gives me a thousand dollars solely to keep his son from inheriting it, I hardly owe him gratitude for his act. And in general we can say that where my benefiting is only an incidental (or even unwanted) consequence of my benefactor's actions, where his real intention was to accomplish some quite different end than an improvement of my lot, no debt of gratitude will be generated by that benefaction.

We have to this point specified that an obligation of gratitude can arise only where a benefit is: 1) granted by means of some special effort or sacrifice, and 2) not granted unintentionally, involuntarily, or for "disqualifying reasons" (as I will call reasons of the sort discussed above). Both these conditions concern the benefactor's role in the "transaction." But there are other conditions which concern instead the desires of the beneficiary.

3. The benefit granted us cannot have been forced on us against our will. I argued for such a condition previously (Chapter V) with my example of the mad scientist who imprisons me in his laboratory and forces on me an injection of a life-extending drug. Although I am benefited immeasurably, no one would hold that I am obligated to

repay the scientist for this. But it is also easy to think of cases in which our intuitions would tend to lead us to the opposite conclusion. Suppose that my closest friend sees that alcohol is driving me to ruin. He takes it upon himself to follow me about, seizing every drink from my hand before I can swallow it; and this goes on for months! Clearly his actions benefit me. In fact, later I acknowledge his determined efforts as the turning point in my life. But at the time, his actions provide me with a benefit that I palpably do not want, and one that is forced upon me against my will. But does it not seem, in spite of this, that my friend has earned my gratitude, if ever a friend has? In both of these examples I receive a significant benefit from another, and in both cases that benefit is forced upon me against my will. What, then, accounts for our feeling that in the second example, but not in the first, I owe my benefactor a debt of gratitude? One obvious difference between the two cases involves the benefactor's concern about the beneficiary. My friend acts out of concern for my welfare while the mad scientist does not. But we can see that this difference between the cases is not crucial by observing that even if the scientist's concern *were* for my welfare, we would still not regard him as being owed a debt of gratitude. For the means he employed in benefiting me were illegitimate. By using *force*, he violated my right to freedom of action, and the mere fact that I would benefit from this violation is not sufficient to justify it. So while I may be glad that my benefactor violated my rights, if he is not justified in doing so, he will be owed nothing by me. He merits no reward for morally prohibited behavior.

On the other hand, there are some sorts of cases in which the paternalistic use of force clearly *is* justified. And one such case is that in which the coerced individual benefits by being prevented from harming himself when he is not fully rational or in control. It is true, I think, that we regard alcoholics as persons not fully in control of themselves, and this may very well be the reason we regard my friend's interference as justified. My friend may be owed a debt of gratitude for his efforts in part because my lack of control justified coercive restraint. If, on the other hand, I could have truly said that I *was* in full control, and *was* fully rational, my friend's interference against my will might have been regarded as unjustified meddling.

I am, of course, aware that this has been a very quick discussion of a very complicated issue. But I do not think that this is the place for discussing the complicated problem of paternalism at length. I present these remarks only by way of showing how our condition 3, as originally stated, must be modified slightly in order to be plausible. Thus, we will want it to read something like: "The benefit granted us cannot have been illegitimately forced on us against our will," or "The benefit granted us cannot have been forced on us against our will unless . . ." (followed by a list of conditions, including, for instance, "unless we are irrational, not in control, not in possession of certain crucial facts," etc.). Of course, the mere fact that the force used *is* legitimate will not establish that the granting of a benefit will generate an obligation. Our other conditions must be satisfied as well.

4. We must want the benefit which is granted.[31] I intend the "want" here to be read in a very broad sense, including a dispositional sense of "want." I intend this condition to allow cases where a person can be *taken to want* the benefit provided; for instance, a man who is run down by a bus on his way to work can be taken to want medical care, even if he is unconscious. And in line with my remarks above (condition 3), I also want as a subcondition (4a) that even if we do not *want* the benefit, it may suffice that we *would want* the benefit if certain "impairing conditions" were corrected (such as drunkenness, mental disorder, certain sorts of ignorance of important facts, etc.). I am certainly aware that it is possible to argue about when a condition is "impairing" in a serious enough way

to engage condition 4a (will immaturity count as an "impairing condition"? or anger?); but it is not necessary for us to solve all of these problems here.

5. We must not want the benefit *not* to be provided *by the benefactor*.[w] Thus, while I may want my lawn to be mowed while I'm out of town, I may *not* want my neighbor to do it; I may prefer not to be indebted to *him*, for a variety of reasons. In fact, I may want my lawn to be mowed without wanting *anyone* to mow it. So the condition that I want the benefit with which I am provided must be supplemented with condition 5.

I should note here that conditions 4 and 5 do not, as it may at first appear, render condition 3 superfluous. For we may want a benefit, and not want it not to be provided by the one who provides it, and still resist being provided with the benefit; we may, for instance, prefer receiving some *other* benefit which cannot be obtained if the first benefit is provided. Thus, condition 3 guarantees that we are not bound to repay benefits granted to us which are provided by means of unjustified force.

We have now set down five necessary conditions for the generation of an obligation of gratitude.

1. The benefit must be granted by means of some special effort or sacrifice.

2. The benefit must not be granted unintentionally, involuntarily, or for disqualifying reasons.

3. The benefit must not be forced (unjustifiably) on the beneficiary against his will.

4. The beneficiary must want the benefit, or, 4a, it must be the case that the beneficiary would want the benefit if certain impairing conditions were corrected.

5. The beneficiary must not want the benefit not to be provided by the benefactor, or, 5a, it must be the case that the beneficiary would not want the benefit not to be pro-

---

[w] Again, as in condition 4, we will want a subcondition, 5a: it must be the case that the beneficiary would not want the benefit not to be provided by the benefactor if certain impairing conditions were corrected.

vided by the benefactor if certain impairing conditions were corrected.

As I have said, I regard these conditions as necessary only; I am not at all sure that they are jointly sufficient. There is, in fact, one condition which may seem to many to be conspicuously absent from the list. It will seem to many that we have forgotten to observe that no debt of gratitude is generated by the provision of benefits which it was the duty or obligation of the benefactor to provide. I have not included this condition for the simple reason that I believe that duty-meeting or obligation-meeting conduct *can* (under certain conditions) generate debts of gratitude. It is significant that the most common sorts of cases in which considerations of gratitude are involved are precisely cases where the benefactor has a duty to grant the benefits in question. Thus, where a passerby aids an accident victim, or more generally where an individual goes to the aid of one in need, his actions seem to be duty-meeting. In helping someone in need, we will normally be doing our duty (although we may of course do more than our duty, or less than our duty): the duty to help those in need. But these seem to be just the sorts of cases in which we think a debt of gratitude is owed to the benefactor.

Let me pursue this line of argument further, trying to show that we can at least sometimes owe debts of gratitude to those who are only doing their duty or discharging an obligation in benefiting us. Suppose that I am driving through the country and come upon an accident victim. I am a medical student and know that if he does not reach a hospital in twenty minutes, he will die. But I also know that the only hospital in the area is twenty miles away over rough back roads. So I drive the victim at sixty miles an hour over rough roads in my brand new Porsche, saving his life and damaging its suspension. Now, I think that there are two things which can truly be said of this case. First, what I did, I had a duty to do; had I ignored the victim, or decided not to risk my Porsche, I would have earned the most serious moral blame. Second, the accident victim has an obligation to compensate me for the damage to my car, if it is within his means. He may have *more* of an obligation to me than this, but this much seems indisputable. And it seems that we can explain this obligation only in terms of gratitude. So here we have a case of duty-meeting conduct generating a debt of gratitude.

We might at first believe, I suppose, that I had somehow done more than my duty, and that gratitude was due for this added service only, not for the duty-meeting conduct itself. It is certainly true that the following situation *could* obtain: in doing A I do my duty, and I am owed a debt of gratitude because I have done A, yet gratitude is *not* due for my duty-meeting conduct. For it may be that in doing A I both do my duty and *more*, and that gratitude is due only for my supererogatory conduct. But in the case under consideration, what aspect of what I have done is supererogatory? Damaging my Porsche? Surely my duty is *not*: to aid those in need provided it costs me nothing. While I may not have a duty to aid a man in need at the risk of my life, the risk of my car's suspension system is another matter.

For those who do not care for the duty to help those in need, I offer the following example. Jones is my very close friend, and knowing that I am likely to want for money for the rest of my life, he makes me an extraordinary promise. He promises to give me $10,000 a year for life, even knowing that this will be a great burden on him. Being a rather unpleasant type, I do not try to turn down his generous offer, but instead accept it. Let us assume that all the conditions necessary for this promise to generate an obligation are satisfied; Jones has an obligation to pay me $10,000 a year, and he does so faithfully. Yet does it not seem that I owe Jones a debt of gratitude for this payment, in spite of the fact that he is obligated to do as he does? I do not see how this can be denied. We might try to say that gratitude is due not for the payment, but for making the promise; but of course making the promise provides no direct benefits in itself, only keeping the promise does this. We might respond that in promising Jones has granted me a right, and that it is this for which gratitude is due. But suppose now that I am not so unpleasant after all, and that the right is no benefit to me, since I would never even dream of trying to enforce it by demanding payment. It seems clear that it is the payment itself for which I owe a debt of gratitude, and that this payment is obligatory.

But while we have shown that obligation or duty-meeting conduct can *sometimes* generate a debt of gratitude, it is clear that even where such conduct provides benefits and meets our five conditions, it does not *always* generate such a debt. I offer two fairly obvious examples. Say that I belong to a club which earns money, and the money is to be distributed in equal amounts to all of the members. The treasurer gives me my share, which he is obligated to do, and provides me with a benefit, satisfying all five of our conditions in doing so. I surely owe him no debt of gratitude, and we will explain this fact by noting that I am entitled to my share. Or, for a second example, suppose that Jones benefits me so that I owe him a debt of gratitude. Later, I provide some benefit to Jones in the course of discharging my debt. There is nothing in what I do which need violate any of our five conditions. Still, no *new* obligation of gratitude arises for Jones as a result of my providing this benefit.

So it seems clear that conduct which both meets our five conditions and is duty- or obligation-meeting, only *sometimes* generates a debt of gratitude. At least frequently, when I provide another with a benefit to which he has a *right*, he will not owe me any debt of gratitude, even if the provision of this benefit satisfies our five conditions. But I confess that I am unable to concoct any clear principle distinguishing cases in which duty-meeting conduct (which satisfies our five conditions) does generate a debt, from those in which it does not. Something which seems

at least relevant to the distinction is the belief that sometimes doing one's duty or discharging one's obligation is
especially praiseworthy. In spite of the longstanding dic-
tum that fulfilling a moral requirement does not deserve
praise, it does seem that some such actions are to be distinguished in a special way. Thus, where the obligation is
undertaken for strongly benevolent reasons, or where the
duty requires not that we refrain from directly harming
another, but rather that we go out of our way to offer
needed assistance, the fulfillment of the requirement
seems to be an action deserving of praise. And it seems
that it is in such cases that obligation- or duty-meeting
conduct can generate debts of gratitude. I regret that I
have nothing clearer to say about this problem.

But before continuing on to a discussion of the "gratitude account" of political obligation, I want to say a few
things about the (alleged) obligations of gratitude owed
by children to parents. As I mentioned previously, it has
been assumed by nearly every writer on the subject of
gratitude that if we believe there are any debts of gratitude
at all, we must certainly believe that children owe them to
their parents (at least, if the parents have not been neg-
lectful). Now, our discussion above may seem to have removed one obstacle to holding that parents are in fact
owed debts of gratitude by their children. It seems clear
that a parent (or guardian) has a *duty* to care for his child,
and it might have seemed that because of this no debt of
gratitude could be incurred for the care a parent gives his
child. But we have also shown that duty-meeting actions
may in fact give rise to such debts. But this, of course, falls
far short of settling the issue, for we have not shown that
all duty-meeting conduct (which satisfies our five conditions) generates obligations of gratitude.

And there are, in fact, reasons to believe that this particular duty-meeting conduct does *not* generate an obligation of gratitude on the child. We suggested previously
that our duties and obligations can only be to perform cer-

tain actions, not to have certain feelings. If this is true, the duty which parents have toward their children can only be a duty to care for them properly, to see that certain opportunities are available to them, and so on. But it cannot be a duty to love them, to "care for them" in the full sense, or to provide the goods for children which depend on having such feelings. Yet when parents do *not* do these things, when they do not provide the benefits of warm and affectionate care which are only possible when the parent *feels* in certain ways, we believe, I think, that *no* gratitude is owed them for the care they give their children. Perhaps the most familiar case along these lines is that in which wealthy parents make sure that their children have all the advantages they need or want, but entrust servants with all the tasks whose performance provides opportunities for the expression of love. In such cases we feel that what is missing from the parent-child relationship is precisely that which may establish ties of gratitude between them. If I am right about this, then it is not simply a routine matter for children to have obligations of gratitude to their parents, nor is the obligation grounded in the mere performance by the parent of his parental duties. And these considerations suggest that it is unwise to use the parent-child model as a paradigm of obligations of gratitude, as so many philosophers have done.

VII.iii. Gratitude as a Ground of Political Obligation

The gratitude account of political obligation maintains that our receipt of the benefits of government binds us to repay the government because of considerations of gratitude. It maintains further that this repayment consists in supporting the government, part of which support consists in obeying the law (this claim, of course, is necessary if the debt of gratitude is to be a *political* obligation). This position has been for the most part ignored by

those who have written on the problem of political obligation. But the results from our general discussion of debts
of gratitude should allow us to evaluate the gratitude account fairly.

Let me begin by mentioning two arguments against the
gratitude account which may have an initial appeal, but
which are in fact unsuccessful. The first argument is
perhaps the most commonly used by those who reject the
gratitude account;[32] we have also considered similar
arguments against the consent theory and fair play accounts. The argument suggests that the gratitude account,
by requiring only the receipt of benefits for the generation
of the obligation, makes it quite easy for us to become
bound to unjust or tyrannical governments (since even
bad governments routinely provide some benefits). And
this seems to some an obviously objectionable consequence. But, in the first place, this argument attacks a
gratitude account not limited by our five conditions. And
even if that were not a problem, I argued in Chapters IV
and V that the possibility of being politically bound to an
unjust government seems an objectionable consequence
of an account only if we believe that obligations cannot be
overridden, or that our political obligations are the only
moral considerations relevant to how we ought to act in
matters political. These views, however, are clearly mistaken. Our being bound to a government by a debt of gratitude would *not* entail that we ought, all things considered, to support and comply with that government. There
may be countervailing obligations or duties which outweigh that debt; and the injustice or cruelty of a bad government's policies will certainly provide strong reasons
for opposing it.

The second initially attractive argument against the
gratitude account maintains that governments have a duty
or a responsibility to provide the benefits which they give
to their citizens, and that citizens have a right to these
benefits. Because of this, the argument continues, no grat-

itude is due. But of course, one of our results in VII.ii was that duty-meeting conduct *can* sometimes generate obligations of gratitude. And while it may still seem possible to press this line of argument (by suggesting that this is *not* such a case), there are other arguments which seem both more fundamental and more obviously successful against the gratitude account.

To begin, there is clearly a problem with the gratitude account which concerns the specification of the content of the obligation which is supposed to be generated. As I noted above, it is not sufficient for the gratitude account of political obligation only to demonstrate the existence of debts of gratitude to the state. This account must also show that the *content* of these debts is such that we will be willing to call them political obligations (for we might have a debt of gratitude to a government with a very different content). In other words, to defeat the gratitude account it would not be necessary to show that citizens do not owe debts of gratitude to their governments; it would suffice to show that even if they did owe such debts, the content of the debts would not be appropriate to giving an account of political obligation. And, remembering our remarks about the "vagueness" of the content of debts of gratitude, this may seem a promising line to take. For we suggested that normally when we acknowledge an obligation of gratitude to another, we are acknowledging only a very general sort of indebtedness. We are normally not bound to any *particular* conduct, except in the case of reimbursing losses incurred by others in the process of benefiting us. On the other hand, if political obligation is to include supporting the government and obeying the law, the obligation would require a very *specific* performance, namely obedience (and this performance could not really be thought of as reimbursement of losses). It seems, then, that political obligation could *not* be an obligation of gratitude; for while supporting the government and obeying the law might be one way of discharging such an obligation of gratitude, it would not be the only way. As M.B.E. Smith notes in his interesting paper, "Is There a Prima Facie Obligation to Obey the Law?":

> It is perhaps true that cheerful and willing obedience
> '   is the best way to show one's gratitude towards gov-
> ernment, in that it makes one's gratitude unmistaka-
> ble. But when a person owes a debt of gratitude to-
> wards another, he does not necessarily acquire a
> prima facie obligation to display his gratitude in the
> most convincing manner. . . . [33]

A likely response to this argument would concede its validity to a limited degree. While it is true, we might say, that a debt of gratitude to the state can be discharged in many ways, there is one *salient* need which a government has. It needs obedience. And because this is not only its foremost need, but one which must be fulfilled in order to maintain its existence, we should pay our debt of gratitude to the government with obedience. This view is espoused by Nannerl Henry: "The reason obedience is the coin in which this particular debt must be paid is that political services cannot be provided unless subjects obey their governments."[34]

But there are simple retorts which show this response to be ineffective. First, even if a debt of gratitude requires that we work toward the fulfillment of a particular need our former benefactor has, it does not require that we do everything in our power to fulfill that need. Thus, by obeying the law often, but not always, I could still be *contributing* to fulfilling the government's need for obedience. But no one would say that our political obligations consisted in obeying the law occasionally! Second, from the fact that our former benefactor has a need which must be fulfilled to maintain his existence, it does not follow that any debt of gratitude to him will require that we work toward fulfilling that need. If Jones was a benefactor to whom I owe a debt of gratitude, and Jones needs to be plugged into a kidney machine all day in order to stay alive, it does not follow that I can discharge my debt to him only by locating, operating, or paying for kidney machines. And from the fact that a government requires obedience in order to subsist, it does not follow that any debt of gratitude to a government can be discharged only by obedience.

But even if the present line of argument seems unconvincing, there are others which also discredit the gratitude account of political obligation. We have to this point been assuming that we *do* owe debts of gratitude to our governments for the benefits they provide, and simply discussing their contents. But there are strong reasons to suppose that we do not owe such debts. Let us see if the provision of the benefits of government to citizens satisfies our five conditions for the generation of obligations of gratitude. We can grant, I suppose, that conditions 3 through 5 are normally satisfied in the relations between citizens and their governments. But it is interesting to note that because of these conditions a gratitude account of political obligation would have to allow that a citizen who could honestly say that he did not want the benefits his government provided, or that he did not want to get them from *his government*, would not be bound by his receipt of benefits.

Conditions 1 and 2, however, cause real problems for the gratitude account. These concern the nature of and reasons for the benefactor's performance. But before I discuss these conditions individually, I want to express some doubts about the gratitude account which center on the role of benefactor; unfortunately, I do not feel able to express these doubts in anything better than very general terms. Put crudely, I feel uncomfortable about attempts to move a principle of gratitude from the realm of interpersonal relations into the realm of benefits provided by institutions. In fact, I have some of the same doubts about benefits provided by groups of persons. And that is because I think that the *reasons* for which a benefit is granted are so crucial to considerations of gratitude.

Where a group of persons is concerned, there is very seldom anything like a reason, common to all of them, for which the benefit was provided. Some members of a group may have worked against providing the benefits, others may have wanted to provide the benefits only to enhance their own positions, and so on. Because of this, it is difficult to know what to say about benefits provided for an individual by a group. But in the case of institutions, the problem is far worse; for institutions are manifestly not complex groups of persons, although we sometimes tend to think of them that way. Can I owe a debt of gratitude to an institution, such as the Ford Foundation, or some university? No doubt there are many past fellows and alumni who think that this is possible. But I suspect that the temptation to believe this rests on thinking of the institution as a group of people, or thinking of particular people whose efforts and generosity made benefits obtained from these institutions possible. To be sure, individuals do fill positions within the structures of institutions. But these positions have functions and the individuals filling them have "positional duties" related to these functions. Insofar as individuals who make these benefits possible are merely "doing their job," considerations of gratitude do not enter the picture at all. But where these individuals make personal sacrifices not required by their jobs, any gratitude due is due not to their positions or to the institutions which define them, but to the individuals in their private capacities. I will have more to say about this momentarily. The general point that I am trying to make is that there may be something illegitimate about an attempt to apply the principle of gratitude to benefits received from (sets of) institutions, such as governments, and perhaps even to those received from groups of persons, such as governors.

But, supposing for argument's sake that such a move is not illegitimate, let us consider now whether the provision of benefits by a government to a citizen satisfies our conditions 1 and 2. It seems clear that it does not. Condition 1 specifies that the benefit must be granted by means of some special effort or sacrifice. But surely, any "sacrifice" which the government makes for me is a very small one. The expense involved in extending the benefits of government to one additional person must be negligible at best. But even if it were not, the fact remains that government services are almost always paid for by citizens through taxes (a fact which struck Benjamin Franklin as a "physical necessity"). And certainly, very little sacrifice is involved in converting these funds into public services.

There may, of course, be individual politicians in government who make great personal sacrifices and whose actions are highly praiseworthy. They may sacrifice personal fortunes and pursue the interests of their constituents or of citizens generally far beyond the requirements of their positions. And, insofar as we benefit from their sacrifices in our interest, we may very well owe them obligations of gratitude. But, as I suggested above, it is important to see that these obligations would not be owed to the *government*, but instead to the individuals in their private capacities. As such, these obligations could not be *political obligations*, which even if owed to the governors rather than to the government, would be owed to some collection of *official* personages.

Condition 2 requires that the benefit not be granted unintentionally, involuntarily, or for disqualifying reasons. Now, it may very well be that the provision of the benefits of government satisfies this condition, but does so *vacuously*; for the ascription of motives to a government may be impossible or incoherent. But insofar as we anthropomorphize governments (or think of the governors as sharing some motive), we would certainly have good reason to be skeptical about the claim that governments do not at least frequently provide benefits to their citizens unintentionally, involuntarily, or for disqualifying reasons.[35] One would think, in fact, that most governmental provisions of benefits fit these categories. We certainly have sufficient experience, even in the best of states, of benefits being conferred as a part of a drive to solicit votes, or to advance the status of the government in international circles, etc.

We have, I think, provided a series of arguments whose combined weight must force us to the conclusion that the gratitude account of political obligation is entirely unsatisfactory. We can, perhaps, imagine governments to which such an account *would* apply. If the very simple absolute monarchy which Hart describes in *The Concept of Law*[36] were ruled by a "Rex" who made significant sacrifices for his subjects, and for the right sorts of reasons (and if our conditions 3 through 5 obtained), we might, I suppose, be willing to call the obligations of gratitude owed him by his subjects "political obligations"; for in such a government there is no separation of private and official capacities. But even if this were true, it would hardly save the gratitude account of political obligation. No such government exists today, nor, as Hart suggests, is it likely that one ever has.

CHAPTER VIII

Concluding Remarks

VIII.i. Political Obligation and Disobedience

We have now concluded our examination of the four accounts of political obligation which I originally recommended as the most plausible, and we have found all four wanting. Of the three principles of obligation which we considered (the principles of consent, fair play, and gratitude), only the principle of consent (with the principle of fidelity) was seen to clearly account for the political obligations of citizens in existing states. But even under this principle only a very few citizens (such as naturalized citizens) seemed to be bound. The other two principles of obligation, while we found them to be valid moral principles, would only seem to bind citizens in states very different from those which presently exist. We also examined Rawls's "Natural Duty of Justice" and found that it was not a useful tool for providing an account of our political bonds. In fact, we concluded that no principles of duty could be helpful in this respect. Even when these four accounts are conjoined, then, they fail to yield a general account of political obligation; very few citizens of existing political communities would be bound even on such a combined account. There is a sense, then, in which our enterprise has reached an unsuccessful end. We have endeavored to present an account of political obligation which is (in the terminology of II.iv) "accurate" and "complete"—an account which picks out those citizens who are bound by special moral ties to their country of residence. But in presenting such an account, we have found that class of citizens to be very limited. The third standard of success in dealing with the problem of political obligation, then, has not been met. We have not been able to present an account which is suitably "general" in its application. And to the extent that we share traditional concerns to meet this third standard, we will find our results disappointing.

The general conclusion to which we are forced by this examination, then, is that political theory cannot offer a convincing general account of our political bonds. For we saw in Chapters I and II that no persuasive alternatives (to the four accounts we have examined) remained. The "particularity requirement" (II.i) eliminated many potential accounts, and we rejected arguments from "positional duty" (I.iii), from the meaning of "law" and "authority" (II.ii), and from utilitarian moral theory (II.iii). We must conclude that citizens generally have no special political bonds which require that they obey and support the governments of their countries of residence. Most citizens have neither political *obligations* nor "particularized" political *duties*, and they will continue to be free of such bonds barring changes in political structures and conventions.

This conclusion is by no means novel. It has been advanced by anarchist thinkers over several centuries. But seldom has this conclusion been the result of a careful or systematic study of the possibilities within the context of traditional liberal political theory, a study undertaken within the constraints of analytic philosophical method. It is uncommon for those (like myself) sympathetic to the liberal tradition to give such a limited role to what has been one of the tradition's central concepts—political obligation. Our work will not seem complete, as a result, without a brief discussion of the significance of this conclusion to political theory. The remainder of this chapter will be devoted to that task. And in the process I will try to tie up loose ends from Chapters II and III concerning the practical import of a theory of political obligation and the legitimacy of governments.

It is likely that many would find our conclusion (that

citizens generally do not have political obligations) objectionable because they believe it to have the following consequence: if citizens do not have political obligations, then they are free to disobey the law whenever they choose. It seems to have been this sort of belief which led Margaret Macdonald to conclude that it was "absurd" that there should be a political society in which the citizens did not have political obligations.[1] And of course, a position which had that consequence *would* be open to attack. But, as I suggested in II.i, from a conclusion that no one in a state has political obligations, *nothing* follows immediately concerning a justification of disobedience. For political obligations are only one factor among many which would enter into a calculation about disobedience. There are, even in the absence of political obligations, still strong reasons for supporting at least certain types of governments and for obeying the law.

For instance, as we suggested in Chapter VI, we have a duty to support and further just government, at least when this involves no great cost to ourselves (as well as a duty to fight injustice). Thus, if our government is just, we will have good reason to support it (and any other just government) even if we have no political obligations. And the other virtues which a government can possess will also be instanced occasionally, providing other reasons for supporting governments possessing them.

Where disobedience to law is concerned, we must remember that disobedience almost always affects someone else negatively, and we have moral duties to those persons, qua persons (as opposed to "citizens"), which must be taken into account. Even where nothing we would want to call a "duty" or an "obligation" is concerned, the effect which our disobedience has on others may provide reasons for obeying. Thus, the existence of a legal order leads people to have certain expectations concerning how others will act. Where, say, disobedience frustrates plans based upon such expectations, there is a *reason* for obedience, even if there is no duty to avoid inconveniencing others. Such reasons will not necessarily be *conclusive*, but they are reasons.

As suggested above, we often have reasons, or even duties, to do what the law requires, quite apart from its being commanded by law. The most important legal prohibitions (i.e., those defining the most serious crimes) concern activities which are morally impermissible—assault, murder, fraud, and theft. But even where the legally prohibited act is not "malum in se," we often have good reason to avoid it, quite independent of its status as legally prohibited. Thus, some laws establish ways of doing things consistently, where inconsistency would be undesirable. Traffic laws provide the best examples. Quite aside from its being illegal to drive on the left, the law has established a rule which, if followed by all, renders driving less hazardous; and while driving on the left is not in itself objectionable, because of the legally created practice of driving on the right we have good reason to obey the law, since disobedience endangers both self and others.

The absence of political obligations within a political community, then, will not *entail* that disobedience or revolution is justified. We will normally have good reasons for obeying the law, and for supporting some types of governments of which our own may be one. But the reasons we have for obeying the law will be the *same* reasons we have for obeying the law when we are in foreign countries. And if we have reason to support our government it will be the *same* reason we have for supporting any other similar government. Thus, the conclusion that most of us have no political obligations does lead to maintaining that we are not *specially* bound to obey *our* laws or to support *our* government, simply because they are ours (or because of what their being ours entails). Insofar as we believe ourselves to be tied in some special way to our country of residence, most of us are mistaken. This is a position which R. P. Wolff associates with what he calls "philosophical anarchism":

When I take a vacation in Great Britain, I obey its laws, both because of prudential self-interest and because of the obvious moral considerations concerning the value of order, the general good consequences of preserving a system of property, and so forth. On my return to the United States, I have a sense of reentering *my* country, and if I think about the matter at all, I imagine myself to stand in a different and more intimate relation to American laws. They have been promulgated by *my* government, and I therefore have a special obligation to obey them. But the anarchist tells me that my feeling is purely sentimental and has no objective moral basis.[2]

It is this position which I believe to follow from my conclusion concerning political obligation. If it runs counter to normal feelings about the citizen-state relationship, I think there are better explanations for this fact than the falsity of my conclusion. For what belief can better serve the interests of one's political leaders than the belief that all are specially bound to support their government and obey the law?

VIII.ii. Political Obligation and Legitimacy

I referred earlier (I.ii and III.i) to the doctrine of the "logical correlativity" of rights and obligations (or duties); the existence of every right is supposed by this doctrine to entail the existence of a corresponding obligation, and vice versa. Specifically, we were concerned with political obligation and the right of the government to command, which have traditionally been supposed to be logical correlates. Thus, the right to command has been thought to be granted the government in undertaking an obligation of obedience to it. Because of this, the problem of governmental legitimacy has also been tied to the problem of political obligation; for if no government is legitimate which does not have de jure political authority, and if having such authority consists in having the right to command and be obeyed, then only where a citizen has political obligations will his government be legitimate with respect to him. Thus, political obligation and governmental legitimacy are also supposed to be correlative notions.

Because of this, another consequence of my conclusion about political obligation is that, at least on traditional models, it involves denying that there are any governments which are legitimate (or which are legitimate with respect to large numbers of citizens). And it may appear that because of this fact we will no longer be able to distinguish between good and bad governments in the way we want, for the political authority which all governments wield now seems to be primarily only *de facto* authority. Traditionally, political theorists have wanted to distinguish between good and bad governments by observing that the former had the *right* to command (and were legitimate), while the latter had only the *power*. But our conclusion that most citizens do not have political obligations renders this method for distinguishing good and bad governments useless, and it may be judged objectionable on that ground.

I am, in fact, quite prepared to accept the conclusion that governments do not normally have the right to be obeyed by their citizens, or to force them to obey, or to punish them for disobedience. Again, it is easy to understand the existence of the widespread belief that governments do have these rights, in terms of the not very subtle policies of political indoctrination to which we are all subjected. But we may also be led to believe that governments have these rights by confusing "having a right" with "being justified" (or "being all right"); I will have more to say about this confusion below.

There are several points which must be made here concerning the conclusion that governments do not have the right to command most of their citizens and are therefore "illegitimate" (in the traditional sense) with respect to most of them. First, this conclusion only strictly follows from our conclusion about political obligation if we accept without question the doctrine of the correlativity of rights and obligations (or duties). I think it is clear that this doctrine is highly questionable,[x] although I confess that it seems quite persuasive in the political case under consideration. Second, we should remember here our earlier discussion of the various senses of "legitimacy" which we use in referring to the status of governments (II.ii). Sometimes in calling a government "legitimate" we refer only to its having come to power in the proper way. Sometimes we call a government "legitimate" if it is a good one (i.e., if it serves the interests of its citizens, does so fairly, remains open to change, etc.), regardless of how it came to power. Or we may call a government "legitimate" if it is recognized internationally, or if its control over a certain domain is effective and unchallenged. None of these senses of "legitimacy" mentions the right to command which we have been discussing as the mark of legitimacy; but all of the "legitimizing features" mentioned above have been taken to *establish* this right.

This, of course, brings us to the approach to political obligation which we discussed in II.ii. Rather than looking for grounds of obligation in the histories of individual citizens, many writers have looked instead to certain good

---

[x] The doctrine of logical correlativity seems most persuasive in the case of what we have called "obligations." As I suggested in I.ii, those moral requirements grounded in the performance of some voluntary act do seem to involve the transfer or creation of correlative rights. But in the case of "duties," the doctrine is unpersuasive. What, for instance, are the rights which correlate with duties of benevolence or charity? While a Rockefeller may have a duty to dispose of his surplus millions charitably, it seems clear that no person or group has a *right* to this performance. For discussions raising other doubts about the correlativity doctrine, see Joel Feinberg, *Social Philosophy*, Prentice-Hall, 1973, chap. 4, and David Lyons, "The Correlativity of Rights and Duties," *Nous* 4 (February 1970). See also, in this context, Hart, "Are There Any Natural Rights?" pt. I, and Feinberg, "Duties, Rights, and Claims," *American Philosophical Quarterly* 3 (April 1966), pt. I.

qualities of government. They have argued that the possession of these qualities establishes both the right to command and the correlative obligation (for all citizens) to obey. In a sense, the approach involves recognizing the *priority* of questions about legitimacy to questions about obligation.[3] But we have already shown that this approach must fail. Any duty which we may have to support our government because of its quality will be "nonparticularized"; that duty may bind us as well to other governments sharing that quality. But in that case, the duty in question cannot bind us to compliance or obedience, and hence cannot bind us to the state in the right way. Further, if the obligation to obey and the right to command *are* logical correlates, then the quality of government *also* cannot establish the right to command. And we saw in Chapter VI (and in section II.ii) that any attempts to "particularize" duties to obey governments with certain good qualities were doomed to failure. The good qualities of my government, then, cannot establish either my obligation to obey it or its right to command me.

What these good qualities *can* do, of course, is to distinguish between governments that *deserve* our support, or that are worthy of it, and those that do not (or are not). It is not the case that simply because governments may all be equal as far as legitimacy (having the right to command) is concerned, that they are all equal. Governments which are just and beneficial, as well as responsive and open to change are not reduced to the level of tyrannical government simply because they share with it "illegitimacy" in the traditional sense. My conclusion does not force us to admit that we can no longer distinguish meaningfully between good and bad governments. Indeed, such distinctions are very seldom drawn in real life on the basis of *rights* which those governments possess or fail to possess. Normally, I think, we rate governments by how well and how fairly they provide the benefits which we expect to receive from government action. And it is in this context that we can see the importance of the "benefits of government," which have been mentioned so often in this essay. We have been concerned since Chapter III to discover the significance of the provision of these benefits to the problem of political obligation. Our conclusion allows us to see that a government's performance in this respect is *not* crucial to settling questions concerning political obligation, but is rather a key factor only in the evaluation of governments. It is easy to understand, of course, how our feelings about the quality of governments may become confused with the recognition of political obligations. But as I argued in Chapter II, if we are to make sense of the notion of political obligation, these two sorts of problems must be kept carefully separate.

This discussion should help us to remember that just as political obligation is only *one* consideration among many in a determination of how we ought to act in matters political, so the right of a government to command and be obeyed is only *one* consideration involved in a justification of government action. Rights and obligations (or duties) do not exhaust the subject matter of morality. It may well be that while a certain government does *not* have the right to command, its actions may nonetheless be morally justifiable; rights violated by its actions may not be as important as other considerations, such as the need for order. Or it may be that a government which *does* have this right would not, under certain circumstances, be morally justified in *exercising* it. There is nothing paradoxical about such conclusions when one frees oneself from the view of morality as a narrow and rigid set of requirements and prohibitions (a view which Kant, more than any other philosopher, impressed upon us). I will not discuss these matters further here, beyond noting that: (a) the moral justifications (of government action) of which I speak are not derivations of, or performed solely in terms of, either a right to command or an obligation to obey; and (b) these considerations seem to suggest that the traditional notion of governmental legitimacy (understood as the possession of a right to command) is not really at the center of the important problems in political philosophy.

In these brief remarks I have tried to show that no in-superable difficulties are involved in my conclusion that most citizens do not have political obligations. But this conclusion does force us to view the position of man in political society in a different way, for it effectively re-moves any *presumption* in favor of obedience to estab-lished authorities. While the absence of political obliga-tions does not justify disobedience, it does force us to discard as a maxim of action: "Other things being equal, obey the political authorities." Obedience remains as much in need of justification as disobedience; for we have no presumption in favor of obedience established by a community-wide obligation to obey. It is in this spirit that we can perhaps understand the (undoubtedly apocryphal) remark attributed to Thoreau during his imprisonment in the county jail of Concord. When asked by Emerson why he was there, Thoreau is supposed to have responded: "Waldo, why are you *not* here?"[4] We are not on "morally safe" ground by obeying the law (as Emerson also recog-nized when he wrote that "good men must not obey the law too well").[5]

For those, like myself, who have always felt uncomfort-able with the suggestion that as citizens we are morally bound in a special way to our own countries, my conclu-sions in this essay may be reassuring. For those who have believed themselves and their fellows bound by such spe-cial obligations, perhaps these remarks can serve as a re-minder that citizenship does not free a man from the bur-dens of moral reasoning. If we have blindly complied in the belief that by doing so we discharged our obligations, we have erred doubly. For, first, most of us have no spe-cial obligation of obedience. But second, even if we had such an obligation, the citizen's job would not be to

blithely discharge it in his haste to avoid the responsibility of weighing it against competing moral claims on his
action. For surely a nation composed of such "dutiful citizens" would be the cruellest sort of trap for the poor, the
oppressed, and the alienated.

Introduction

1. Kurt Baier, "Obligation: Political and Moral," in J. R. Pennock and J. W. Chapman (eds.), *Nomos XII: Political and Legal Obligation*, Atherton, 1970, p. 116.

2. Thomas McPherson, *Political Obligation*, Routledge & Kegan Paul, 1967, esp. chaps. 8 and 9.

Chapter I: Obligations

1. See, for example, H.L.A. Hart, "Legal and Moral Obligation," in A. Melden (ed.), *Essays in Moral Philosophy*, University of Washington Press, 1958, p. 95, and Joel Feinberg, "Duties, Rights, and Claims," *American Philosophical Quarterly* 3 (April 1966). How this connection with pressure and coercion is to be explained remains a live issue in moral philosophy. H.L.A. Hart has examined the relation between obligation and coercion at great length (in *The Concept of Law*, Oxford University Press, 1961, esp. chap. V), and at one point argued that an obligation *justified* the use of coercion to insure performance of the obligation ("Are There Any Natural Rights?" *Philosophical Review* 64 [1955], p. 178). Hart was followed in this view by Kurt Baier ("Moral Obligation," *American Philosophical Quarterly* 3 [July 1966], pp. 223-224) and D.A.J. Richards (*A Theory of Reasons for Action*, Oxford University Press, 1971, p. 98). But see Robert Nozick's reply in *Anarchy, State, and Utopia*, Basic Books, 1974, pp. 91-92.

2. This century's moral philosophers have not been exceptions. W. D. Ross seems to confuse (a), (b), (c), and (e) in *The Right and the Good*, Oxford University Press, 1967, pp. 3-4, and in *Foundations of Ethics*, Oxford University Press, 1930, p. 43. Similarly, H. A. Prichard equates (a),

(b), and (c) in "Moral Obligation" (in *Moral Obligation and Duty and Interest*, Oxford University Press, 1968), pp. 147-148. More recently, John Ladd seems at one point or another to run all five of these types of judgments together in "The Distinctive Features of Obligation-Statements," *Journal of Philosophy* 53 (October 25, 1956), while A. Berry Crawford inexplicably asserts the equivalence of (a) and (e), as well as that of (b) and (c), in "On the Concept of Obligation," *Ethics* 79 (July 1969).

3. This was first pointed out by C. H. Whiteley in his important paper "On Duties," *Proceedings of the Aristotelian Society* 53 (1952-53). His observations were seconded and expanded upon by H.L.A. Hart ("Legal and Moral Obligation" and "Are There Any Natural Rights?"), Joel Feinberg ("Supererogation and Rules," *Ethics* 71 [July 1961]), and E. J. Lemmon ("Moral Dilemmas," *Philosophical Review* 71 [April 1962]).

4. Lemmon, "Moral Dilemmas."

5. Feinberg, "Supererogation and Rules," pp. 275-277.

6. Ibid., pp. 278-279.

7. As James K. Mish'Alani has suggested, in " 'Duty,' 'Obligation,' and 'Ought,' " *Analysis* 30 (December 1969), p. 39.

8. R. B. Brandt, "The Concepts of Obligation and Duty," *Mind* 73 (July 1965).

9. On the notion of a "responsibility," see Feinberg, "Duties, Rights, and Claims," p. 141, and Mish'Alani, " 'Duty,' 'Obligation,' and 'Ought,' " p. 34.

10. Here I follow Mish'Alani, " 'Duty,' 'Obligation,' and 'Ought,' " pp. 34-35.

11. The "natural duties" are discussed by Rawls in sections 19 and 55 of *A Theory of Justice*, Harvard University Press, 1971, and in Richards, *A Theory of Reasons for Action*, chaps. 7-10. I refer the reader to these sources for more complete discussions of matters I touch on only in passing.

12. Hart, "Are There Any Natural Rights?" p. 179, note 1.

13. Brandt, "The Concepts of Obligation and Duty," p. 378.

14. Hart, "Are There Any Natural Rights?" pp. 183-184.

15. Joel Feinberg discusses the variety of rights and their correlative moral requirements in "Duties, Rights, and Claims."

16. Michael Stocker, "Moral Duties, Institutions, and Natural Facts," *The Monist* 54 (October 1970), p. 603.

17. Ibid., pp. 606-607.

18. This has, of course, been only the sketch of an argument. I have left much unsaid and asserted more than I have effectively argued for. I refer the reader to Stocker's paper and the work of Rolf Sartorius (most recently in his *Individual Conduct and Social Norms*, Dickenson, 1975) for more complete discussions of the problem and of the hard cases which face the position I defend. See also J. R. Cameron, " 'Ought' and Institutional Obligation," *Philosophy* 46 (October 1971), and Brandt, "The Concepts of Obligation and Duty," pp. 380-384, and "Some Merits of One Form of Rule-Utilitarianism," *University of Colorado Series in Philosophy*, No. 3 (1967), sec. IX.

19. Haskell Fain, "The Idea of the State," *Nous* 6 (March 1972), p. 25.

20. Many writers on the subject have failed to observe these distinctions. Richard Taylor, for example, seems to confuse legal obligations with political obligations: "A political obligation, therefore, is a duty defined by the law of the state" (*Freedom, Anarchy, and the Law*, Prentice-Hall, 1973, p. 75). Carl Cohen, on the other hand, conflates positional "duties of citizenship" and political obligations, in *Civil Disobedience*, Columbia University Press, 1971, pp. 5-6.

21. For an illuminating discussion of "prima facie" requirements (and many of the other problems dealt with in this chapter), see Sartorius, *Individual Conduct and Social Norms*, chap. 5.

22. Ross, *The Right and the Good*, p. 18, note 1.

23. Ibid., p. 20.

24. Ibid., p. 28.

25. Here I follow Harry Beran's remarks in "Ought, Obligation, and Duty," p. 214.

26. For instance, P. F. Strawson's refutation of the argument from "tendencies to be right (or obligatory)," in "Ethical Intuitionism," *Philosophy* 24 (January 1949).

27. Russell Grice seems to accept this view in *The Grounds of Moral Judgement*, pp. 31-32, as does John Rawls in *A Theory of Justice*, pp. 340-341. Others who hold similar views are H. J. McCloskey, "Ross and the Concept of a Prima Facie Duty," *Australasian Journal of Philosophy* 41 (December 1963), and Crawford, "On the Concept of Obligation."

28. Hart, "Are There Any Natural Rights?" p. 186.

Chapter II: The Problem of Political Obligation

1. Certainly the classical political theorists—like Hobbes, Locke, Rousseau, and Kant—all held to the strong connection. But many contemporary works also include commitments to the strong connection. See, e.g., Richard Flathman, *Political Obligation*, Atheneum, 1972, esp. chap. 2, secs. II, III, and IV; Michael Walzer, *Obligations: Essays on Disobedience, War, and Citizenship*, Simon and Schuster, 1971, chap. 1; Hanna Pitkin, "Obligation and Consent—II," *American Political Science Review* 60 (March 1966).

2. For instance, John Ladd in "Legal and Moral Obligation," in Pennock and Chapman (eds.), *Nomos XII: Political and Legal Obligation*.

3. For discussions of Socrates's arguments in *Crito*, see A. D. Woozley, "Socrates on Disobeying the Law," in G. Vlastos (ed.), *The Philosophy of Socrates*, Doubleday, 1971; and Flathman, *Political Obligation*, chap. 8.

4. Ladd, "Legal and Moral Obligation," p. 27.

5. See, e.g., McPherson, *Political Obligation*, pp. 21-22; Baier, "Obligation: Political and Moral," p. 117; J. P.

Plamenatz, *Consent, Freedom, and Political Obligation*, 2nd ed., Oxford University Press, 1968, p. 3.

6. Joseph Tussman, *Obligation and the Body Politic*, Oxford University Press, 1960.

7. See the subsequent discussions in II.ii, III.iv, and VIII.ii.

8. For a brief discussion of Green's "idealist" theory of political obligation and its relation to other idealist theories (e.g., those of Hegel and Bosanquet), see Clifford L. Barrett, *Ethics*, Harper & Bros., 1933, chap. XII.

9. "Green's Principles of Political Obligation," in Prichard's *Moral Obligation and Duty and Interest*.

10. See, for instance, McPherson, *Political Obligation*.

11. Flathman, *Political Obligation*, chap. 3. Similar lines are suggested in McPherson, *Political Obligation*, chap. 7, and John R. Carnes, "Why Should I Obey the Law?" *Ethics* 71 (October 1960), pp. 16-21.

12. Pitkin, "Obligation and Consent—II," p. 49.

13. Ibid., p. 48.

14. On the distinction between "de facto" and "de jure" notions of authority, see R. S. Peters, "Authority," and Peter Winch, "Authority," both in *Proceedings of the Aristotelian Society*, Supp. Vol. 32 (1958); R. P. Wolff, *In Defense of Anarchism*, Harper and Row, 1970, chap. 1; S. I. Benn and R. S. Peters, *Social Principles and the Democratic State*, George Allen & Unwin, 1959, chap. 14.

15. I owe this example to Nicholas Sturgeon.

16. This problem was discussed in II.i and will be taken up again in Chapter VI.

17. Bentham, *A Fragment on Government*, chap. I, secs. 36-48.

18. J. S. Mill, *On Liberty*, chap. 1, par. 11.

19. Sidgwick actually describes himself not as a "utilitarian," but as a "Utilitarian on an Intuitional basis," both in *Outlines of the History of Ethics*, 6th ed., Beacon, 1968, p. 301, and in the preface to the 6th edition of *The Methods of Ethics*. He discusses the problem of political obligation very briefly (in connection with Intuitionism)

in bk. III, chap. VI of *The Methods of Ethics*, 7th ed., Dover, 1966.

20. Bentham, *A Fragment on Government*, chap. I, sec. 43.

21. It is worth noting here that the act-utilitarian's employment of rules of thumb may not be entirely in accord with the spirit of act-utilitarianism. See Bernard Williams's discussion in section 6 of "A Critique of Utilitarianism" in B. Williams and J.C.C. Smart, *Utilitarianism: For and Against*, Cambridge University Press, 1973.

22. Sartorius, *Individual Conduct and Social Norms*.

23. Ibid., pp. 101-109.

24. For an account of some of these problems, see Alan Goldman, "Can a Utilitarian's Support of Nonutilitarian Rules Vindicate Utilitarianism?" *Social Theory and Practice* 4 (Fall 1977).

25. Sartorius presents a useful summary of the main arguments against rule-utilitarianism in *Individual Conduct and Social Norms*, pp. 11-18. See also the well-known arguments in David Lyons, *Forms and Limits of Utilitarianism*, Oxford University Press, 1965; J.C.C. Smart, "An Outline of a System of Utilitarian Ethics," in Williams and Smart, *Utilitarianism: For and Against*; B. J. Diggs, "Rules and Utilitarianism," *American Philosophical Quarterly* 1 (January 1964), and "A Comment on 'Some Merits of One Form of Rule-Utilitarianism,' " in K. Pahel and M. Schiller (eds.), *Readings in Contemporary Ethical Theory*, Prentice-Hall, 1970.

26. For a brief discussion of "ideal-rule utilitarianism" and the obligation to obey the law, see M.B.E. Smith, "Is There a Prima Facie Obligation to Obey the Law?" *Yale Law Journal* 82 (1973), section III.

27. Jonathan Harrison, "Utilitarianism, Universalization, and our Duty to be Just," *Proceedings of the Aristotelian Society* 53 (1952-53). Harrison, admittedly, supports this interpretation of Hume at least largely because he thinks Hume would be better off with the view he ascribes to him.

28. John Rawls, "Two Concepts of Rules," *Philosophical Review* 64 (1955).

29. See especially, *A Treatise of Human Nature*, bk. III, pt. II, sec. II (par. 23, sentence 3), and bk. III, pt. II, sec. VII (par. 3). Many other passages in Hume, including the famous analogy of the vault (in Appendix III to *An Enquiry Concerning the Principles of Morals*) support this reading.

30. *Treatise*, bk. III, pt. II, sec. X.

Chapter III: The Consent Tradition

1. David Hume, "Of the Social Contract."

2. For discussions of these two notions of political authority, see R. S. Downie, *Roles and Values*, Methuen, 1971, chap. 4, sec. 3, and Benn and Peters, *Social Principles and The Democratic State*, chap. 14.

3. Romans, 13:1 and 2.

4. John Chapman has characterized this reaction as the replacement of the "moral functionalism" of medieval natural law theories, with a "moral individualism" which stressed human rights (in "The Moral Foundations of Political Obligation," in Pennock and Chapman [eds.], *Nomos XII: Political and Legal Obligation*). What made the theory of natural rights (and consent theory) possible was the increasing secularization of natural law, whereby duties began to be conceived of as owed to one's fellows rather than exclusively to God.

5. For discussions of these early "consent theories," and of social contract theory generally, see D. G. Ritchie, "Contributions to the History of the Social Contract Theory," in *Darwin and Hegel*, Macmillan, 1893, and J. W. Gough, *The Social Contract*, Oxford University Press, 1936.

6. The "Vindiciae" was a Huguenot pamphlet whose authorship has never been conclusively determined.

7. J. W. Gough, *John Locke's Political Philosophy*, 2nd ed., Oxford University Press, 1973, p. 59.

8. Buchanan's *De jure regni apud Scotos* (Da Capo,

1969), first published in 1579, argued that political obligation was conditional on the sovereign's just performance of his duties, and that the king's power was conditional on the community's consent.

9. Richard Hooker, *Of the Laws of Ecclesiastical Polity* (E. P. Dutton & Co., 1925), written between 1594 and 1597. Hooker's influence on Locke's conceptions of natural law and political obligation are well known.

10. Johannas Althusius, *Politica methodice digesta* (Harvard University Press, 1932), first published in 1603.

11. Hugo Grotius, *De jure belli ac pacis* (published as *The Rights of War and Peace*, M. W. Dunne, 1901), first published in 1625.

12. John Milton's *The Tenure of Kings and Magistrates* (in *Prose Works: 1641-1650*, Scolar, 1967) defends the execution of Charles I, the natural right to resist a tyrant, and the "natural freedom" of man. As an illustration that consent theory is not logically tied to any particular political views, it is worth remembering that Milton was bitterly opposed to the theory of the state espoused by Hobbes, another consent theorist.

13. For a detailed study of this period of political thought, I recommend George H. Sabine's *A History of Political Theory*, Henry Holt & Co., 1937, chaps. XVIII-XXVI. It remains, despite its age, the best "complete" history of political philosophy available.

14. For instance, in *On the Old Saw*, University of Pennsylvania Press, 1974, pp. 65, 69-70, and in *The Metaphysics of Morals*, pt. I (or *The Metaphysical Elements of Justice*, Bobbs-Merrill, 1965), sec. 49.

15. Locke defends this claim in spirited fashion in his *Second Treatise of Government*, sections 112-118.

16. Margaret Macdonald discusses these problems with the theory of historical consent in "The Language of Political Theory," in A.G.N. Flew (ed.), *Logic and Language*, 1st series, Blackwell, 1963, p. 178.

17. Rousseau, *Social Contract*, I.i.

18. For a good discussion both of natural rights and the

natural right of freedom, see Hart's "Are There Any Natural Rights?" I follow Hart's account closely.

19. For instance, see the opening to the *Constitution of Massachusetts*: "All men are born free and equal, and have certain natural, essential, and inalienable rights." Here being "born free and equal" seems to amount, in fact, to nothing more than having these rights.

20. Hobbes, *Leviathan*, chap. 14. Hobbes's "Right of Nature," of course, turns out to be a mere "liberty" (the absence of restricting obligation), not a "right" in the full sense. And this liberty may not, in fact, be limited by any natural moral constraints (although this remains a point of controversy in Hobbes scholarship).

21. Locke, *Second Treatise of Government*, sec. 4.

22. Kant, *The Metaphysics of Morals*, pt. I, Introduction. See his similar remarks in *On the Old Saw*, p. 59.

23. Hart, "Are There Any Natural Rights?" p. 183. I use the term "special obligation" to denote those obligations which correlate with Hart's "special rights."

24. As Hobbes notes: "there is no obligation on any man which ariseth not from some act of his own," in *Leviathan*, chap. 21.

25. *Leviathan*, chap. 14.

26. On this argument, see Alan Gewirth, *Political Justice*, in R. B. Brandt (ed.), *Social Justice*, Prentice-Hall, 1962, p. 129.

27. *Social Contract*, I.vi.

28. *The Metaphysics of Morals*, pt. I, Appendix.

29. *De Cive*, chap. III, sec. 7.

30. *Leviathan*, chap. 15.

31. Ibid., chap. 14.

32. *Second Treatise of Government*, sec. 135. The same point is made more forcefully in sec. 23.

33. *On the Old Saw*, p. 61.

34. Ibid., p. 72.

35. Sidgwick, *The Methods of Ethics*, p. 298.

36. *Leviathan*, chap. 14.

37. For instance, see Kant, *On the Old Saw*, pp. 60-61.

38. For a discussion of this "spirit of individualism" and how it directs one approach to the problem of political obligation, see Tussman, *Obligation and the Body Politic*, esp. pp. 17-18.

39. Austin, *How to Do Things with Words*, Lecture II.

40. Gewirth, "Political Justice," p. 135.

41. *Social Contract*, IV.ii.

42. *Leviathan*, chap. 18.

43. *Second Treatise of Government*, secs. 95-98.

44. Hobbes, *Leviathan*, "A Review and Conclusion"; Locke, *Second Treatise of Government*, sec. 119; Rousseau, *Social Contract*, IV.ii.

Chapter IV: The Argument from Tacit Consent

1. Plamenatz, *Consent, Freedom, and Political Obligation*, p. 3.

2. Here I follow, to a certain extent, Hart's discussion in "Are There Any Natural Rights?" p. 184.

3. See especially J. R. Searle, *Speech Acts*, Cambridge University Press, 1970, chap. 3.

4. *A Theory of Justice*, p. 343.

5. Ibid., p. 112.

6. Ibid., p. 343.

7. *Leviathan*, chap. 14.

8. Some of the following points are suggested by J.F.M. Hunter's remarks in "The Logic of Social Contracts," *Dialogue* 5 (June 1966).

9. For a thorough discussion of Locke on consent, see J. P. Plamenatz, *Man and Society*, Longmans, Green & Co., 1963, vol. I, 220-241.

10. *Second Treatise of Government*, sec. 119.

11. Ibid.

12. Ibid.

13. "Obligation and Consent—I," *American Political Science Review* 59 (December 1965), p. 995.

14. *Second Treatise of Government*, sec. 23.

15. "Obligation and Consent—I," p. 995.

16. Ibid., p. 996.

17. *Second Treatise of Government*, sec. 23.

18. Ibid., secs. 135, 137, 149, 171, 172.

19. Ibid., sec. 122.

20. Meiklejohn argues that "as fellow citizens we have made and are continually remaking an agreement with one another, and . . . , whatever the cost, we are in honor bound to keep that agreement." The agreement amounts to "a voluntary compact among political equals." Both quotations are from Alexander Meiklejohn, *Free Speech and Its Relation to Self-Government*, Harper & Bros., 1948, pp. 14, 11.

21. Gewirth's position does not really appear to be that by participating in political processes we give our consent. Rather, he holds that consent consists somehow in the availability of certain political options. I confess that I find his account somewhat confusing. He writes: "The consent which is a necessary condition of political obligation is not primarily the consent of determinate individuals occurring at specifiable times; it is rather the maintenance of a method which leaves open to every sane, noncriminal adult the opportunity to discuss, criticize, and vote for or against the government" ("Political Justice," p. 138). For an effective criticism of Gewirth's arguments on consent, see Smith, "Is There a Prima Facie Obligation to Obey the Law?" sec. II.

22. *Consent, Freedom, and Political Obligation*, pp. 168, 170.

23. Ibid., p. 171.

24. For other criticisms of Plamenatz's arguments, see Marshall Cohen, "Liberalism and Disobedience," *Philosophy and Public Affairs* 1 (Spring 1972), pp. 311-312; Smith, "Is There a Prima Facie Obligation to Obey the Law?" sec. II; Frederick Siegler, "Plamenatz on Consent and Obligation," *Philosophical Quarterly* 18 (July 1968). E. F. Carritt also disputes the claim that voting is a sign of consent, in *Morals and Politics*, Oxford University Press, 1935, p. 215.

25. "Are There Any Natural Rights?" pp. 185-186.

26. John Rawls, "Legal Obligation and the Duty of Fair Play," in S. Hook (ed.), *Law and Philosophy*, New York University Press, 1964.

27. *Consent, Freedom, and Political Obligation*, p. 24.

28. Hart seems to have this point in mind in "Are There Any Natural Rights?" p. 186.

29. *Social Contract*, IV.ii.

30. Ross, *The Right and the Good*, p. 27.

31. Plato, *Crito*, 51d-e.

32. See, e.g., Plamenatz, *Consent, Freedom, and Political Obligation*, p. 7, and Gough, *John Locke's Political Philosophy*, p. 70.

33. There could be, as Pitkin notes ("Obligation and Consent—I," p. 995), no such thing as "tacit dissent," short of emigration. Some contemporary consent theorists, like Michael Walzer, try to incorporate something like "tacit dissent" in their theories. See Walzer, *Obligations*, chaps. 3 and 5.

34. Tussman, *Obligation and the Body Politic*, p. 38.

35. David Hume, "Of the Original Contract," in A. MacIntyre (ed.), *Hume's Ethical Writings*, Collier-Macmillan, 1965, p. 263. A. C. Ewing seems to be making a similar point when he observes that there is no real "voluntary bargain" made with the state for the benefits it confers: "I could not have refused the benefits conferred by the state except by committing suicide or emigrating" (A. C. Ewing, *The Individual, the State, and World Government*, Macmillan, 1947, p. 217).

Chapter V: The Principle of Fair Play

1. The principle was given this name in John Rawls's essay "Legal Obligation and the Duty of Fair Play," in Hook (ed.), *Law and Philosophy*. Similar, but unnamed, principles had been previously discussed in C. D. Broad, "On the Function of False Hypotheses in Ethics," *International Journal of Ethics* 26 (April 1916), and in Hart, "Are

There Any Natural Rights?'' (see below). On the utilitarian's difficulties with fair play, see David Lyons, *Forms and Limits of Utilitarianism*, Oxford University Press, 1965, chap. V.

2. "Are There Any Natural Rights?" p. 185.

3. Ibid.

4. Ibid., pp. 190-191.

5. Actually, Rawls gives at least four different accounts of the principle of fair play. His first, in "Justice as Fairness" (*Philosophical Review* 68 [April 1958]), follows Hart's account exactly, with the exception of an added requirement that participants in the practice "accept its rules as fair" (p. 179). I will discuss Rawls's 1964 account. Later versions, in "The Justification of Civil Disobedience" (in H. Bedau [ed.], *Civil Disobedience: Theory and Practice*, Pegasus, 1969) and *A Theory of Justice*, do not differ substantially from the 1964 account.

6. "Legal Obligation and the Duty of Fair Play," pp. 9-10.

7. Ibid., p. 10.

8. Hart, "Are There Any Natural Rights?" p. 185.

9. Rawls, *A Theory of Justice*, p. 112.

10. Ibid., p. 343.

11. Ibid., p. 112.

12. John Ladd, "Legal and Moral Obligation," in Pennock and Chapman (eds.), *Nomos XII: Political and Legal Obligation*, p. 21.

13. This point is made clearly in Hart's account of the principle.

14. Nozick, *Anarchy, State, and Utopia*, pp. 90-95. Nozick calls the principle "the principle of fairness," using Rawls's more recent name for it.

15. Ibid., p. 93.

16. Ibid., p. 94.

17. Ibid.

18. Ibid., pp. 94-95.

19. Ibid., p. 95.

20. Ibid., p. 94.

21. Ibid., p. 95.
22. Ibid., p. 94.
23. Rawls, *A Theory of Justice*, p. 112.
24. Rawls, "Legal Obligation and the Duty of Fair Play," p. 17.
25. Hart, "Are There Any Natural Rights?" pp. 185-186.
26. Perhaps Rawls would not accept the need to give "microlevel" support for a principle to be applied on a "macrolevel." See Nozick's discussion of these points in *Anarchy, State, and Utopia*, pp. 204-206. But it is doubtful that the principle of fair play can even be understood as a principle for the macrostructure of society.

Chapter VI: The Natural Duty of Justice

1. Rawls, *A Theory of Justice*, p. 114.
2. John Rawls, "The Justification of Civil Disobedience," in Bedau (ed.), *Civil Disobedience: Theory and Practice*.
3. *A Theory of Justice*, pp. 336-337.
4. Ibid., p. 334.
5. Ibid.
6. "The Justification of Civil Disobedience," p. 241.

Chapter VII: Gratitude

1. Jeffrie G. Murphy, "In Defense of Obligation," in Pennock and Chapman (eds.), *Nomos XII: Political and Legal Obligation*, pp. 42-43.
2. Ewing, *The Individual, the State, and World Government*, p. 218.
3. Kurt Baier makes a similar point in "Obligation: Political and Moral" (in *Nomos XII: Political and Legal Obligation*, p. 130).
4. Plato, *Crito*, 50d-51d.
5. Ewing, *The Individual, the State, and World Government*, p. 218.

6. Ross, *The Right and the Good*, p. 27.

7. Plamenatz, *Consent, Freedom, and Political Obligation*, p. 24.

8. Ross regards the "duty of gratitude" as one of the seven important "prima facie duties" (*The Right and the Good*, p. 21).

9. D.A.J. Richards discusses the "obligation to return good" in chap. 9 of *A Theory of Reasons for Action*. Another recent discussion, which I follow in several respects, is Fred Berger's "Gratitude," *Ethics* 85 (July 1975).

10. Daniel Lyons, "The Odd Debt of Gratitude," *Analysis* 29 (January 1969), p. 92.

11. David Hume, *A Treatise of Human Nature*, bk. III, pt. I, sec. I.

12. Immanuel Kant, *Lectures on Ethics*, Harper & Row, 1963, p. 218.

13. Hobbes, *Leviathan*, chap. 15.

14. Richard Price, *A Review of the Principal Questions in Morals*, chap. VII.

15. Kant, *The Metaphysics of Morals*, pt. II, sec. 32.

16. Henry Sidgwick, *The Methods of Ethics*, 7th ed., Dover, 1966, p. 259.

17. John Balguy, *The Foundations of Moral Goodness*, pt. II, art. V.

18. Ibid., art. IV.

19. Kant, *The Metaphysics of Morals*, pt. II, sec. 31.

20. Ross, *The Right and the Good*, pp. 22-23.

21. Sidgwick, *The Methods of Ethics*, p. 261.

22. Berger, "Gratitude," p. 299.

23. Kant mentions "the profit and advantage which the person obligated has derived from the benefit" and "the disinterestedness with which it was bestowed" as the two key variables; but he also mentions effort as a prominent consideration (in *The Metaphysics of Morals*, pt. II, sec. 33).

24. As Sidgwick at one point suggests (and later, apparently, rejects): "we think perhaps that an equal return

is what the duty of gratitude requires" (*The Methods of Ethics*, p. 260).

25. Ibid., p. 261.

26. On this point and those immediately following, see Berger, "Gratitude," esp. p. 299.

27. P. F. Strawson, "Freedom and Resentment," in P. F. Strawson (ed.), *Studies in the Philosophy of Thought and Action*, Oxford University Press, 1968, pp. 75-76.

28. Nozick, *Anarchy, State, and Utopia*, p. 95.

29. Ibid.

30. As Nicholas Sturgeon has pointed out to me.

31. Sidgwick makes some remarks which support this view, although he does not actually ever state it concisely: "the benefit may be altogether unacceptable, and it is hard to bind us to repay in full every well-meant blundering effort to serve us . . ." (*The Methods of Ethics*, p. 261).

32. See, for example, Richard Flathman's *Political Obligation*, where it is argued that "past benefits are not a sufficient ground of political obligation" because if they were, we could become bound to obey "the Nazi regime" by taking benefits from it (pp. 270-280).

33. Smith, "Is There a Prima Facie Obligation to Obey the Law?" Smith discusses gratitude in section I of his paper.

34. Nannerl O. Henry, "Political Obligation and Collective Goods," in Pennock and Chapman (eds.), *Nomos XII: Political and Legal Obligation*.

35. For a strong expression of this view, see Michael Walzer, "The Problem of Citizenship," chap. 10 in *Obligations: Essays on Disobedience, War, and Citizenship*.

36. Hart, *The Concept of Law*, chap. IV, sec. i.

Chapter VIII: Concluding Remarks

1. Margaret Macdonald, "The Language of Political Theory," in A.G.N. Flew (ed.), *Logic and Language*, 1st series, Blackwell, 1963, p. 184.

2. Wolff, *In Defense of Anarchism*, pp. 18-19.

3. These two approaches to the problem of political obligation (and the problem of political authority) are discussed in Rex Martin's "Two Models for Justifying Political Authority," *Ethics* 86 (October 1975).

4. Thoreau's views on the justification of disobedience are defended, rather unsystematically, in his famous essay "Civil Disobedience." He writes: "I think that we should be men first, and subjects afterward. It is not desirable to cultivate a respect for the law, so much as for the right."

5. Emerson, "Politics."

Abbate, Fred. *A Preface to the Philosophy of the State.* Wadsworth, 1977.

Althusius, Johannes. *Politica methodice digesta.* Harvard University Press, 1932.

Austin, J. L. *How to Do Things with Words.* Oxford University Press, 1970.

Baier, Kurt. "Moral Obligation." *American Philosophical Quarterly* 3 (July 1966).

———. "Obligation: Political and Moral," in J. R. Pennock and J. W. Chapman (eds.), *Nomos XII: Political and Legal Obligation.* Atherton, 1970.

Balguy, John. *The Foundations of Moral Goodness.* Garland, 1976.

Barrett, Clifford. *Ethics.* Harper & Bros., 1933.

Benn, S. I., and R. S. Peters. *Social Principles and the Democratic State.* George Allen & Unwin, 1959.

Bentham, Jeremy. *A Fragment on Government,* in J. Bowring (ed.), *The Works of Jeremy Bentham.* Simpkin, Marshall & Co., 1843.

———. *An Introduction to the Principles of Morals and Legislation,* in Bowring.

———. *Truth versus Ashhurst,* in Bowring.

Beran, Harry. "In Defense of the Consent Theory of Political Obligation and Authority." *Ethics* 87 (April 1977).

———. "Ought, Obligation, and Duty." *Australasian Journal of Philosophy* 50 (December 1972).

———. "Political Obligation and Democracy." *Australasian Journal of Philosophy* 54 (December 1976).

Berger, Fred. "Gratitude." *Ethics* 85 (July 1975).

Berlin, Isaiah. "Does Political Theory Still Exist?" in P. Laslett and W. G. Runciman (eds.), *Philosophy, Politics, and Society,* second series, Blackwell, 1962.

Bowie, Norman, and Robert Simon. *The Individual and the Political Order.* Prentice-Hall, 1977.

Brandt, R. B. *Ethical Theory*. Prentice-Hall, 1959.

―――. "The Concepts of Obligation and Duty." *Mind* 73 (July 1965).

―――. "Some Merits of One Form of Rule-Utilitarianism." *University of Colorado Series in Philosophy*, No. 3 (1967).

Broad, C. D. "On the Function of False Hypotheses in Ethics." *International Journal of Ethics* 26 (April 1916).

Brownsey, P. F. "Hume and the Social Contract." *Philosophical Quarterly* 28 (April 1978).

Buchanan, George. *De jure regni apud Scotos*. Da Capo, 1969.

Cameron, J. R. " 'Ought' and Institutional Obligation." *Philosophy* 46 (October 1971).

Carnes, John. "Why Should I Obey the Law?" *Ethics* 71 (October 1960).

Carritt, E. F. *Morals and Politics*. Oxford University Press, 1935.

Chapman, John. "The Moral Foundations of Political Obligation," in J. R. Pennock and J. W. Chapman (eds.), *Nomos XII: Political and Legal Obligation*. Atherton, 1970.

Childress, James. *Civil Disobedience and Political Obligation*. Yale University Press, 1971.

Cohen, Carl. *Civil Disobedience*. Columbia University Press, 1971.

Cohen, Marshall. "Liberalism and Disobedience." *Philosophy and Public Affairs* 1 (Spring 1972).

Crawford, A. Berry. "On the Concept of Obligation." *Ethics* 79 (July 1969).

D'Entreves, A. P. *Natural Law*. Hutchinson & Co., 1972.

―――. "Legality and Legitimacy." *The Review of Metaphysics* 16 (June 1963).

―――. "Obeying Whom." *Political Studies* 13 February 1964).

―――. "On the Nature of Political Obligation." *Philosophy* 43 (October 1968).

Diggs, B. J. "Rules and Utilitarianism." *American Philosophical Quarterly* 1 (January 1964).

———. "A Comment on 'Some Merits of One Form of Rule-Utilitarianism,'" in K. Pahel and M. Schiller (eds.), *Readings in Contemporary Ethical Theory*. Prentice-Hall, 1970.

Downie, R. S. *Roles and Values*. Methuen, 1971.

Dworkin, Gerald. "Paternalism," in R. Wasserstrom (ed.), *Morality and the Law*. Wadsworth, 1971.

Emerson, Ralph Waldo. "Politics," in B. Atkinson (ed.), *The Complete Essays and Other Writings of Ralph Waldo Emerson*. Random House, 1940.

Ewing, A. C. *The Individual, the State, and World Government*. Macmillan, 1947.

Fain, Haskell. "The Idea of the State." *Nous* 6 (March 1972).

Feinberg, Joel. *Social Philosophy*. Prentice-Hall, 1973.

———. "Duties, Rights, and Claims." *American Philosophical Quarterly* 3 (April 1966).

———. "The Nature and Value of Rights." *Journal of Value Inquiry* 4 (Winter 1970).

———. "Supererogation and Rules." *Ethics* 71 (July 1961).

Flathman, Richard. *Political Obligation*. Atheneum, 1972.

Gewirth, Alan. "Political Justice," in R. B. Brandt (ed.), *Social Justice*. Prentice-Hall, 1972.

Goldman, Alan. "Can a Utilitarian's Support of Nonutilitarian Rules Vindicate Utilitarianism?" *Social Theory and Practice* 4 (Fall 1977).

Gough, J. W. *John Locke's Political Philosophy*, 2nd ed. Oxford University Press, 1973.

———. *The Social Contract*. Oxford University Press, 1936.

Green, T. H. *Lectures on the Principles of Political Obligation*. Ann Arbor Paperbacks, 1967.

Grice, Russell. *The Grounds of Moral Judgement*. Cambridge University Press, 1967.

Grotius, Hugo. *De jure belli ac pacis (The Rights of War and Peace)*. M. W. Dunne, 1901.

Harman, Gilbert. *The Nature of Morality*. Oxford University Press, 1977.

Harrison, Jonathan. "Utilitarianism, Universalization, and our Duty to be Just," *Proceedings of the Aristotelian Society* 53 (1952-53).

Hart, H.L.A. *The Concept of Law*. Oxford University Press, 1961.

———. "Are There Any Natural Rights?" *Philosophical Review* 64 (April 1955).

———. "Legal and Moral Obligation," in A. I. Melden (ed.), *Essays in Moral Philosophy*. University of Washington Press, 1958.

Henry, Nannerl. "Political Obligation and Collective Goods," in J. R. Pennock and J. W. Chapman (eds.), *Nomos XII: Political and Legal Obligation*. Atherton, 1970.

Hobbes, Thomas. *De Cive*, in B. Gert (ed.), *Man and Citizen*. Doubleday, 1972.

———. *Leviathan*. Bobbs-Merrill, 1958.

Honderich, Ted. *Political Violence*. Cornell University Press, 1976.

Hooker, Richard. *Of the Laws of Ecclesiastical Polity*. E. P. Dutton & Co., 1925.

Hume, David. *An Enquiry Concerning the Principles of Morals*, in A. MacIntyre (ed.), *Hume's Ethical Writings*. Collier-Macmillan, 1965.

———. *A Treatise of Human Nature*. Oxford University Press, 1968.

———. "Of the Social Contract," in MacIntyre.

Hunter, J.F.M. "The Logic of Social Contracts." *Dialogue* 5 (June 1966).

Jenkins, J. "Political Consent." *Philosophical Quarterly* 20 (January 1970).

Johnson, Conrad. "Moral and Legal Obligation." *Journal of Philosophy* 72 (June 19, 1975).

Johnson, Karen. "Political Obligation and the Voluntary Association Model of the State." *Ethics* 86 (October 1975).

Kant, Immanuel. *On the Old Saw*. University of Pennsylvania Press, 1974.

————. *Lectures on Ethics*. Harper & Row, 1963.

————. *The Metaphysics of Morals*, Part II: *The Metaphysical Principles of Virtue* and Part I: *The Metaphysical Elements of Justice*. Bobbs-Merrill, 1964, 1965.

Kaplan, Morton. *Justice, Human Nature, and Political Obligation*. Free Press, 1976.

Ladd, John. "The Distinctive Features of Obligation-Statements." *Journal of Philosophy* 53 (October 25, 1956).

————. "Legal and Moral Obligation," in J. R. Pennock and J. W. Chapman (eds.), *Nomos XII: Political and Legal Obligation*. Atherton, 1970.

Ladenson, Robert. "Legitimate Authority." *American Philosophical Quarterly* 9 (October 1972).

LeBaron, Bentley. "Real and Mythic Obligations." *Ethics* 78 (October 1967).

Lemmon, E. J. "Moral Dilemmas." *Philosophical Review* 71 (April 1962).

Lemos, Ramon. "Assassination and Political Obligation," in H. Zellner (ed.), *Assassination*. Schenkman, 1974.

Locke, John. *Two Treatises of Government*. Cambridge University Press, 1960.

Lyons, Daniel. "The Odd Debt of Gratitude." *Analysis* 29 (January 1969).

Lyons, David. *Forms and Limits of Utilitarianism*. Oxford University Press, 1965.

————. "The Correlativity of Rights and Duties." *Nous* 4 (February 1970).

————. "Human Rights and the General Welfare." *Philosophy and Public Affairs* 6 (Winter 1977).

Macdonald, Margaret. "The Language of Political

Theory," in A.G.N. Flew (ed.), *Logic and Language*, first series. Blackwell, 1963.

MacPherson, C. B. *The Political Theory of Possessive Individualism*. Oxford University Press, 1962.

Manicas, Peter. *The Death of the State*. Capricorn, 1974.

Martin, Rex. "Two Models for Justifying Political Authority." *Ethics* 86 (October 1975).

McCloskey, H. J. "Ross and the Concept of a Prima Facie Duty." *Australasian Journal of Philosophy* 41 (December 1963).

McPherson, Thomas. *Political Obligation*. Routledge & Kegan Paul, 1967.

Meiklejohn, Alexander. *Free Speech and Its Relation to Self-Government*. Harper & Bros., 1948.

Melden, A. I. *Rights and Persons*. University of California Press, 1977.

———. *Rights and Right Conduct*. Blackwell, 1959.

Mill, J. S. *On Liberty*, in M. Warnock (ed.), *Utilitarianism and Other Writings*. Meridian, 1962.

———. *Utilitarianism*, in Warnock.

Milton, John. *The Tenure of Kings and Magistrates*, in *Prose Works, 1641-1650*. Scolar, 1967.

Mish'Alani, James. " 'Duty,' 'Obligation,' and 'Ought.' " *Analysis* 30 (December 1969).

Moore, G. E. *Principia Ethica*. Cambridge University Press, 1968.

Morris, Herbert. "Persons and Punishments." *Monist* 52 (October 1968).

Murphy, Jeffrie. "In Defense of Obligation," in J. R. Pennock and J. W. Chapman (eds.), *Nomos XII: Political and Legal Obligation*. Atherton, 1970.

Nozick, Robert. *Anarchy, State, and Utopia*. Basic Books, 1974.

Pennock, J. R. "The Obligation to Obey the Law and the Ends of the State," in S. Hook (ed.), *Law and Philosophy*. New York University Press, 1964.

Peters, R. S., and S. I. Benn. *Social Principles and the Democratic State*. George Allen & Unwin, 1959.

————. "Authority." *Proceedings of the Aristotelian Society*, Supp. Vol. 32 (1958).

Pitkin, Hanna. "Obligation and Consent, I and II." *American Political Science Review* 59, 60 (December 1965, March 1966).

Plamenatz, J. P. *Consent, Freedom, and Political Obligation*, 2nd ed. Oxford University Press, 1968.

————. *Man and Society*. Longmans, Green & Co., 1963.

Plato. *Crito*, in E. Hamilton and H. Cairns (eds.), *Plato: Collected Dialogues*. Princeton University Press, 1969.

Price, Richard. *A Review of the Principal Questions in Morals*. Oxford University Press, 1974.

Prichard, H. A. "Green's Principles of Political Obligation," in *Moral Obligation and Duty and Interest*. Oxford University Press, 1968.

————. "Moral Obligation," in *Moral Obligation and Duty and Interest*.

Raphael, D. D. *Problems of Political Philosophy*. Macmillan, 1976.

Rawls, John. *A Theory of Justice*. Harvard University Press, 1971.

————. "Justice as Fairness." *Philosophical Review* 68 (April 1958).

————. "The Justification of Civil Disobedience," in H. Bedau (ed.), *Civil Disobedience: Theory and Practice*. Pegasus, 1969.

————. "Legal Obligation and the Duty of Fair Play," in S. Hook (ed.), *Law and Philosophy*. New York University Press, 1964.

————. "Two Concepts of Rules." *Philosophical Review* 64 (1955).

Reiman, Jeffrey. *In Defense of Political Philosophy*. Harper & Row, 1972.

Rescher, Nicholas. *Distributive Justice*. Bobbs-Merrill, 1966.

Richards, D.A.J. *A Theory of Reasons for Action*. Oxford University Press, 1971.

Ritchie, D. G. "Contributions to the History of the Social Contract," in *Darwin and Hegel*. Macmillan, 1893.

Ross, W. D. *Foundations of Ethics*. Oxford University Press, 1930.

———. *The Right and the Good*. Oxford University Press, 1967.

Rousseau, Jean Jacques. *Social Contract*. Everyman, 1950.

Ruben, David-Hillel. "Tacit Promising." *Ethics* 83 (October 1972).

Sabine, George. *A History of Political Theory*. Henry Holt & Co., 1937.

Sartorius, Rolf. *Individual Conduct and Social Norms*. Dickenson, 1975.

Searle, J. R. *Speech Acts*. Cambridge University Press, 1970.

Seliger, Martin. *The Liberal Politics of John Locke*. George Allen & Unwin, 1968.

Shope, Robert. "Prima Facie Duty." *Journal of Philosophy* 62 (May 27, 1965).

Sibley, Mulford. *The Obligation to Disobey*. C.R.I.A., 1970.

———. "Conscience, Law, and the Obligation to Obey." *Monist* 54 (October 1970).

Sidgwick, Henry. *The Methods of Ethics*, 7th ed. Dover, 1966.

———. *Outlines of the History of Ethics*, 6th ed. Beacon, 1968.

Siegler, Frederick. "Plamenatz on Consent and Obligation." *Philosophical Quarterly* 18 (July 1968).

Simmons, A. John. "Tacit Consent and Political Obligation." *Philosophy and Public Affairs* 5 (Spring 1976).

———. "The Principle of Fair Play." *Philosophy and Public Affairs* 8 (Summer 1979).

Simon, Robert, and Norman Bowie. *The Individual and the Political Order*. Prentice-Hall, 1977.

Singer, Peter. *Democracy and Disobedience*. Oxford University Press, 1974.

Smart, J.C.C. "An Outline of a System of Utilitarian Ethics," in B. Williams and J.C.C. Smart, *Utilitarianism: For and Against*. Cambridge University Press, 1973.

Smith, M.B.E. "Is There a Prima Facie Obligation to Obey the Law?" *Yale Law Journal* 82 (1973).

Stocker, Michael. "Moral Duties, Institutions, and Natural Facts." *Monist* 54 (October 1970).

Strawson, P. F. "Ethical Intuitionism," *Philosophy* 24 (January 1949).

———. "Freedom and Resentment," in P. F. Strawson (ed.), *Studies in the Philosophy of Thought and Action*. Oxford University Press, 1968.

Taylor, Richard. *Freedom, Anarchy, and the Law*. Prentice-Hall, 1973.

Thoreau, Henry D. "Civil Disobedience," in H. Bedau (ed.), *Civil Disobedience: Theory and Practice*. Pegasus, 1969.

Tussman, Joseph. *Obligation and the Body Politic*. Oxford University Press, 1960.

Walzer, Michael. *Obligations: Essays on Disobedience, War, and Citizenship*. Simon and Schuster, 1971.

Wasserstrom, Richard. "The Obligation to Obey the Law." *U.C.L.A. Law Review* 780 (1963).

Welden, T. D. *The Vocabulary of Politics*. Penguin, 1953.

Whiteley, C. H. "On Duties." *Proceedings of the Aristotelian Society* 53 (1952-53).

Williams, Bernard. "A Critique of Utilitarianism," in B. Williams and J.C.C. Smart, *Utilitarianism: For and Against*. Cambridge University Press, 1973.

Winch, Peter. "Authority." *Proceedings of the Aristotelian Society*, Supp. Vol. 32 (1958).

Wolff, R. P. *In Defense of Anarchism*. Harper & Row, 1970.

Woozley, A. D. "Socrates on Disobeying the Law," in

G. Vlastos (ed.), *The Philosophy of Socrates*. Double-
day, 1971.
Young, Gary. "Authority." *Canadian Journal of Philoso-
phy* 3 (June 1974).
Zwiebach, Burton. *Civility and Disobedience*. Cambridge
University Press, 1975.

INDEX

LIBRARY OF CONGRESS CATALOGING IN PUBLICATION DATA

Simmons, Alan John, 1950-
   Moral principles and political obligations.

   Bibliography: p.
   Includes index.
   1. Allegiance.   2. Justice.   3. Political ethics.
I. Title
JC328.S55   323.6'5'01   79-2505
ISBN 0-691-07245-0
ISBN 0-691-02019-1 pbk.